MW01609540

Canadian Colonialism

PAST AND PRESENT

Boris W. Kishchuk

FriesenPress

Suite 300 - 990 Fort St
Victoria, BC, V8V 3K2
Canada

www.friesenpress.com

Copyright © 2021 by Boris W. Kishchuk

First Edition — 2021

With editorial assistance by Natalie A. Kishchuk

Cover Photo Credits:
Photograph of Children
Source: Provincial Archives of Saskatchewan
Photograph No. R-B11388
Photograph of Internees
Source: University of Calgary Archives and Special Collections.
Glenbow Archives Photograph NA-1870-6

All rights reserved.

No part of this publication may be reproduced in any form, or by any means, electronic or mechanical, including photocopying, recording, or any information browsing, storage, or retrieval system, without permission in writing from FriesenPress.

ISBN
978-1-03-910289-7 (Hardcover)
978-1-03-910288-0 (Paperback)
978-1-03-910290-3 (eBook)

1. POLITICAL SCIENCE, COLONIALISM & POST-COLONIALISM

Distributed to the trade by The Ingram Book Company

Table of Contents

Preface

WHILE SOME CANADIANS HAVE STUDIED THE HISTORY OF THEIR COUNTRY, many might not know that the Battle of the Plains of Abraham between Britain and France took place in 1759, nor that this battle was only one of several being fought as part of the Seven Years' War. Few would be able to identify 1763 as the year that France officially ceded its land claims in Canada to the British. Some might know that a number of First Nations signed treaties with Canada (actually with the Queen of the United Kingdom of Great Britain and Ireland), but they might not know the terms of the treaties or that 350,000 unwed Canadian mothers were coerced to give up their babies for adoption only sixty years ago.

Canada was born as a colony of two competing world powers with some of their colonial attitudes and actions becoming embedded in the new nation. For example, the passing of The Indian Act in 1876 ensured that the Canadian government has control over a specific segment of its population, thus creating a second class of citizens. By contrast, we do not have an English Act or a Scottish Act or an Italian Act.

This book is about examining a part of Canada's history. It is about how Canadians treated each other in the development of Canada as a democratic and fair country. In many instances, this treatment has been less than desirable. Yet Canada is today considered one of the best countries in the world in which to live, as anyone who has travelled or lived in other countries can attest. So why bring up its "dirty laundry"? The answer is that undesirable actions in the treatment of some of its citizens has occurred in the not-so-distant past and some acts of colonialism remain present at this time. Many of those affected by colonialism are alive today and are scarred for life.

This book discusses a number of instances where the government took action against the symptoms of a problem instead of examining and acting upon its root cause. This was particularly true in dealing with Canada's Indigenous populations in such issues as the Chilcotin War in British Columbia in 1864, the Indigenous conflicts in Saskatchewan in 1885 and the relocation of the Quebec Inuit peoples to the High Arctic in 1953 and 1955. In the cases of the Indian Residential School System, the internment of Japanese Canadians in World War Il and Canadians of eastern-European origin in World War I, the government acted in a colonial manner without consultation or reflection on the consequences of its actions. People caught up in the Sixties Scoop program or forcefully required to give up their newborn children continue to suffer the consequences to this day. It is somewhat ironic that Canada, a product of a colony itself, should practice colonialism.

Internal colonialism is complex with many facets. The purpose of this book is not to propose solutions to the problems created by colonialism in Canada. Indeed, each of the communities covered in the chapters of this book has its own pathway forward, whether through reconciliation, reparation, decolonialization, activism, or the courts. My intent is educational: to know and understand our history by drawing together a series of disparate instances of internal colonialism across Canada's post-colonization history and to shed some light on their consequences. Why, for instance, is the suicide rate among First Nations Canadians three times higher than non-Indigenous Canadians, or why did Japanese Canadians imprisoned in internment camps during World War II not tell their children about their experiences?

Book Genesis and Format

To answer these questions, I decided to study the issues. I first became aware of the Indian Residential Schools a number of years ago when an acquaintance mentioned in a casual conversation that he had attended a residential school. In a later conversation, he mentioned that while at the school he was abused, and when he left school, he turned to alcohol to try to forget his experiences. When the report of the Truth and Reconciliation

Commission was published, documenting the extent of the exploitation that had occurred in the schools, I decided to continue my research and subsequently to write this book

When I began writing, I was already familiar with the World War I internment of Canadians who had emigrated from eastern Europe. My grandparents were from Ukraine, but they were listed as citizens of Austria-Hungary when they entered Canada and theoretically could have been labelled as enemy aliens. Subsequent inquiry helped me identify many more instances of Canadian internal colonialism. The presentation of examples included in this book groups them according to three major themes: colonialism by forced uprooting and displacement; by direct attack and subjugation; and by disdain, disrespect, and denial of rights.

Introduction

Canadian Colonialism

THERE ARE SEVERAL DIFFERENT DEFINITIONS OR MEANINGS FOR COLOnialism. Although they are similar, some are more precise. The definition that will be used in this book is the one cited in the Stanford Encyclopedia of Philosophy, which defines colonialism as "the practice of domination, which involves the subjugation of one people to another."[1]

There are a number of types of colonialism: *exploitation colonialism; settler colonialism; and internal colonialism.*[2] The colonialism of Central and South America by the Spaniards and other European countries in the 1700s and 1800s was *exploitation colonialism.* It focused on the exploitation of natural resources such as gold and the exploitation of indigenous populations for labour purposes. Wealth so accumulated was transferred back to the colonizing country with very little remaining in the new colony.

The colonization of North America by the British and French was *settler colonialism.* It involved large-scale migration and actual settlement of people in the new colony. Settler colonialism can be motivated by religious, political, or economic reasons or a combination of all of these. Colonies of immigrant peoples are established to survive on a permanent basis.

The focus of this book is *internal colonialism.* As defined for our purposes here, it occurs when there is an uneven distribution of power and authority among the inhabitants of the country. The source of exploitation comes from within the state when one segment controls another segment, using a variety of lawful and unlawful means. Internal colonialism can be triggered by factors such as economic exploitation, religious bias, and political considerations. Internal colonialism may also be the by-product of settler colonialism as the new masters practice the colonialism of their past masters.

Intertwined with the practice of colonialism is that of racism. Racism can be executed by governments, government agencies, public institutions, or individuals. At all of these levels, the consequences of racism can have the same negative effects. The definition of racism used here is from the Oxford English Dictionary: "Racism is the belief that all members of each race possess characteristics, abilities, or qualities specific to that race, especially so as to distinguish it as inferior or superior to another race or races."[3]

Terminology

The terminology used in chapters dealing with Canadian Indigenous Peoples requires some explanation, as word usage has been changing in recent years. For example, the word "Indian" is no longer being used (or used to a lesser extent), except in the legal sense, to identify a person who lived in Canada before European invasion and settlement.

The terminology identified by Bob Joseph in his book *21 Things You May Not Know about the Indian Act*[4] will be used:

- Indigenous Peoples: Peoples referred to as Indian, Inuit, and Metis.
- Aboriginal Peoples: Defined in the Constitution Act, 1982, to include all Indigenous Peoples of Canada: Indian, Metis, and Inuit.
- First Nation: Used to replace the term Indian Band. It is not applied to Inuit or Metis, who are distinct and separate.
- First Nations Peoples: used to identify those individuals who are legally identified as status or non-status Indians in Canada.

Section 1

Colonialism by Forced Uprooting and Displacement

Chapter 1

Indian Residential and Day Schools

THE ESTABLISHMENT OF INDIAN RESIDENTIAL SCHOOLS IN CANADA WAS one of the most grievous acts of internal colonialism carried out by the Canadian government in its history. The schools, funded by the federal government and operated by Christian churches, were established to integrate Indigenous children into Euro-Canadian culture at the expense of their own family's native language, customs, and spiritual beliefs. In total, an estimated 150,000 First Nation, Inuit, and Metis children forcibly attended residential schools. While the schools went through a number of different forms, the intent was consistent—assimilation.

To assist in understanding the implementation and operation of the Indian Residential Schools in Canada and to understand why they had such a devastating impact on the individuals who attended and their families, some historical perspective is given.

Canadian Indigenous Peoples

Origins

There is general acceptance of the theory that the Indigenous Peoples of Canada are of Asian origin and migrated onto the continent from what is now Siberia. There is still some question about when this migration occurred, but recent archaeological discoveries indicate human existence on the continent as early as 16,000 years ago.[5]

During the last ice age, sea and ocean water levels around the North American continent were lower than now as much of the earth's water was contained in the glaciers. There was a land connection between the Asian and North American continents at what is now Siberia and Alaska respectively. This land mass was identified as Beringia. At the same time, there was a ground-exposed corridor between two parallel north-south glaciers covering North America. This corridor allowed migrating peoples to enter into the central North America continent. There was also a sea route along the shores of what is now British Columbia for Asian migrants to follow in their quest for new sources of food.[6]

Indigenous Settlement in Canada

Before the arrival of Europeans in Canada, the whole of the country was settled by many distinct communities that Europeans grouped into two categories of Indigenous Peoples – the First Nations and the Inuit. The First Nations consisted of some 600 separate nations that spoke over fifty different languages. The Inuit lived in what is now referred to as the Arctic and High Arctic regions of Canada. The land was sparsely populated, but there were continuous settlements from the eastern Atlantic coast to the western Pacific coast and into the High Arctic. As wild animals and fish were the main foods, the relatively low-density population ensured overhunting and overfishing did not generally occur, creating relatively stable sources.[7]

Spiritual Beliefs of First Nations

At the time the Indian Residential Schools were being established, the First Nations approach to spirituality and religion was markedly different from that of the Europeans who emigrated and settled in Canada. According to First Nation author Blair Stonechild in his book *The Knowledge Seeker*, First Nations people's belief is that humans are not the centre of Creation but are only one entity in the created world and that all entities, such as animals, plants, soils, and minerals, are interconnected and rely on one another to exist. Humans exist because of the sacrifices of other entities such as animals that are killed for food and grains that are harvested for sustenance. First Nation people's beliefs are that all entities must be treated with respect.

With respect to the difference between spirituality and religion, Stonechild offers this explanation: "An important distinction is to be made between spiritualty and religion. *Spirituality* involves direct engagement and connection with the mysteries of the transcendent. It is the responsibility of each individual to pursue this enterprise. *Religion* is characterized by a belief system defined in rigid written texts, such as the Torah, Bible, or Koran. The ordinary person's relationship with the sacred is mediated by interpreters, be they priests or rabbi."[8]

A First Nations elder explains the First Nations approach to spirituality as follows: "We do not have a religion, but rather a way of living that includes prayer and worship. The Indian way is not a religion but a way of understanding the spiritual world. The teacher is the spirit, who comes to us through thoughts and the actions of others. It is a close relationship with the Creator in all aspects of our lives. Ceremonies allow for meditation. Aboriginal spirituality is open to anyone who is interested."[9]

Structure and Education of First Nations Families

Family structures among First Nations varied, but all were different from that of the European settlers. Generally, First Nations families were structured around spirituality, kinship, and economic conditions while European societies were built around nuclear families.

According to Blair Stonechild, First Nations human development is embedded in a family structure where spirituality is of prime importance. A maturing person passes through six phases in a mentorship process that is provided in a family setting by parents, grandparents, other family members, and elders.[10] Kinship plays a large role in First Nation families as do economic circumstances. For example, prior to the arrival of Europeans, some First Nations were matrilocal (where the husband goes to live with the wife's family) in nature while others were patrilocal (where the wife joins the husband's family), depending on their economic situation.[11]

Without the availability of a written language, knowledge, history, language, skills, and spirituality were passed on to the succeeding generation verbally and usually at the family and kinship levels. In cases of disruption in the mentoring structure, important knowledge of skills and history was lost to successive generations.

Effects of European Settlement

Food Shortages and Disease

Food shortages and disease that came with settlement had major impacts on the lives and well-being of First Nations peoples. Food shortages resulted in malnutrition, which in turn, created increased susceptibility to disease.

Diseases brought by Europeans onto the North American continent severely affected the Indigenous populations, who had no immunity to them. First Nations who lived close to French colonies in eastern Canada were, as early as the 1630s, exposed to strains of measles, influenza, and smallpox with devastating effects.[12] The spread of smallpox travelled west, and by the 1780s, entire First Nations entities had disappeared.[13] As the fur trade expanded, so did the spread of fatal diseases, from both the south and the east. In an 1837-38 smallpox epidemic that took place along the Missouri River where First Nation communities straddled the U. S. and Canadian border, an estimated 17,000 First Nations peoples died.[14] The spread of communicable disease that proved fatal to the Indigenous populations continued into the twentieth century, when severe outbreaks of tuberculosis occurred.[15]

Traditionally, Indigenous Peoples lived off the land that was available to them. As such, they were aware of the necessity to preserve the balance of need and availability. The influx of Europeans upset that balance, in particular with the bison population.

First Nation peoples in the western part of the continent hunted bison as their main food source as well as for supplies for clothing and shelter. Because of overhunting by both Canadians and Americans, the bison population began to decrease rapidly in the mid-1850s. In the winter of 1873-74, it was reported that "Cree at the Victoria mission near the present Alberta–Saskatchewan border were reduced to eating their horses, dogs, and buffalo robes and then died."[16] By 1878, the bison hunt in Canada had collapsed completely. Canadian government officials were aware of the potentially disastrous consequences of a decline in the bison population as early as 1874. The Deputy Director of the Interior reported: "The buffaloes have, in last few years, been rapidly diminishing in numbers, and there seems every reason to expect… they will within the next decade of years be entirely eliminated. To the Indians, extermination of the buffalo means starvation and death."[17]

The Treaties

The Canadian government recognizes seventy so-called historic treaties that were signed between 1701 and 1923. These treaties include:

- Treaties of Peace and Neutrality (1701 – 1760)
- Peace and Friendship Treaties (1725 – 1779)
- Upper Canada Land Surrenders and the Williams Treaties (1764 – 1862/1923)
- Robinson Treaties and Douglas Treaties (1850 – 1854)
- The Numbered Treaties (1871 – 1921)[18]

The early treaties were signed between First Nations and the British government, which was representing the British monarchy. One of the purposes of the first group of treaties was to co-opt the First Nations to fight with the British against the French. The second group of treaties affected territories that became southern Ontario. The main purpose of those treaties was to gain ownership of the lands occupied by the First Nations. In one case, a parcel of land was surrendered for 300 suits of clothing.[19] After Confederation in 1867, with the construction of the transcontinental railway and migration of Europeans west, there was more urgency in securing lands occupied by the First Nations. The "numbered" treaties began in 1871 with Treaty No. 1, covering an area of southern

Manitoba. The bulk of western Canada was surrendered by First Nations to Canada by Treaties Nos. 2 to 7. The last of the treaties, Numbers 8 to 11, were signed some years later as resource extraction began in the northern areas, including the Northwest Territories. In total, the treaties affected 364 of 617 First Nations, representing now over 600,000 First Nations peoples in Canada.[20]

As J. R. Miller points out in his book *Skyscrapers Hide the Heavens,* the First Nation treaty negotiators were at a disadvantage during negotiations due to language considerations and their differing beliefs from those of the government negotiators. For example, to them "the land and its resources were the creation of the Great Spirit, and the Indian was but one inhabitant of the world with obligations to use the resources prudently and pass them on to succeeding generations undiminished. They could not negotiate surrender of title because they did not possess it. What the Indians sought in the negotiations in the 1870s was the establishment of a relationship with the Dominion of Canada that would offer them assurances for the future, while agreeing to permit entry and some settlement in the region. To them, the treaties were intended to be pacts of friendship, peace, and mutual support: they did not constitute the abandonment of their rights and interests."[21] As will be noted in Chapter 10, a court decision issued in 2014 sided with the First Nations in this regard.

To add to their disadvantage during the years that the numbered treaties were being negotiated, the First Nations were under considerable stress. As noted previously, they were suffering from malnutrition, and in some cases, starvation due to the demise of the bison. In addition, much of the population was being decimated by disease, especially smallpox and tuberculosis.

In general, the numbered treaties required that the First Nations "cede, release, surrender and yield up" their rights to the land in exchange for reserves (small parcels of communal land, usually of marginal value), cash payments, ammunition, fishing twine, uniforms, medals for the chiefs, annual payments to each First Nation as well as to each member, and promises of continued hunting and fishing rights. But from the First Nations perspective, there were differences between what they were told they were signing and the actual written documents. "Gifts such as flags and medals enhanced the illusion that these were pacts of friendship and mutual assistance, when in fact they were primary deeds of sale."[22]

The First Nations were well aware of the changes that were taking place in their traditional ways of life as a result of the occupation of their territories by European immigrants. They knew the importance that education would play for future generations. As a result, the numbered treaties required the Canadian Government to be responsible for providing education on the reserves that were being established. For example, Treaties Nos. 1 and 2 stated: "And further, Her Majesty agrees to maintain a school in each reserve hereby made whenever the Indians of the reserve shall desire it." Treaty No. 6 states: "And further, Her Majesty agrees to maintain schools for instruction in such reserves hereby made as to Her Government of the Dominion of Canada may seem advisable, whenever the Indians of the reserve shall desire it."[23]

However, notwithstanding its obligations under the treaties, the government developed the Indian Residential School System that required First Nations students to attend schools off reserves and some distances away from their family homes rather than have children attend schools that operated on reserve land. The government's intent was to isolate the children from their parents and families and begin the process of assimilation into the Euro-Canadian culture and beliefs.

Establishment of the Indian Residential Schools System

The Doctrine of Discovery

The establishment of the Indian Residential Schools in Canada is based on the belief and use of colonialism as a tool in directing and controlling a group of people. Colonialism is based on the concept of the Doctrine of Discovery, established in fifteenth-century Europe. At that time, Europe consisted of major powers including Spain, Portugal, England, and France, each of which wanted to expand its territories and wealth. Those countries, under the influence of the Roman Catholic Papacy, created the Doctrine of Discovery in their search for new territories and wealth, with the non-Catholic countries willingly following suit.

In 1493, Pope Alexander VI issued "the first of four orders (papal bulls) that granted most of North and South America to Spain, the kingdom that sponsored Christopher Columbus's voyages the preceding year."[24] The basis of the Pope's orders was that "[t]he Christian God had given the Christian nations the right to colonize the lands they 'discovered' as long as they converted the Indigenous populations, and secondly, the Europeans were bringing the benefits of civilization to the 'heathen.' In short, it was contended that people were being colonized for their own benefit, either in this world or the next."[25]

The presence of Christian missionaries in occupied countries throughout the world provided a cover for the occupiers. They were there to spread the word of God, but at the same time, they worked to destroy existing family traditions and the culture and spiritual beliefs of the Indigenous Peoples.

Government Attitude, Policy, and Actions

The seeds of establishing boarding and industrial schools for the Indigenous Peoples began in Canada as early as 1842, while Canada was still a British colony. The then governor general of Canada, Sir Charles Bagot, appointed a commission to report on "the Affairs of the Indians in Canada." The commission recommended an assimilationist policy, including the establishment of boarding schools distant from the child's community, to provide training in manual labour and agriculture.[26] The probable model for the initial industrial schools in Canada was based on developments that were taking place in Britain, where the Industrial Schools Act was passed in 1857. The intent of the British Act was to house and educate the children of the urban poor in industrial schools, away from their families.[27]

Prior to the establishment of residential schools in Canada, Christian missionaries began opening boarding schools for First Nations children. For example, in the 1820s, John West, an Anglican missionary from England, opened a boarding school at Red River, Ontario. Similarly, a mission boarding school on the Grand River in Ontario was opened in

1834 and Methodist missionaries operated a number of boarding schools in southern Ontario in the 1850s.[28] The first missionary boarding schools in British Columbia were established in 1861: St. Mary's Mission Indian Residential School and the Presbyterian Coqualeetza Indian Residential School at Chilliwack. The first missionary boarding school on the prairies, Blue Quills Indian Residential School, was established at St. Paul, Alberta, in 1862.[29] One of the first Roman Catholic missionary boarding schools was established in Fort Providence, Northwest Territories, in 1867. After confederation, in 1867, the Canadian Government started to provide small per-student grants to many of the church-run boarding schools.[30]

The government began plans to develop the residential school system for First Nations in a more systematic way in 1878 with a report by the Deputy Minister of the Department of the Interior, J.S. Dennis, to Prime Minister Sir John A. Macdonald. Dennis advised "that the long-term goal should be to instruct our Indian and half-breed populations in farming, raising cattle, and the mechanical trades, rendering them self-sufficient." In Dennis's view, this would "pave the way for their emancipation from tribal government, and for their absorption into the general community."[31] Dennis's report was followed by one prepared by Nichols Davin. Based on his research of schools in the United States, he advised that the government should develop a residential school system on the prairies that would be directed toward the destruction of Aboriginal spirituality. To accomplish this, he recommended that the government fund the schools but that the churches operate them.[32]

The government decided to proceed on the basis of Davin's report and agreed to open three industrial schools, which were later called residential schools. The first two were in what is now Saskatchewan. The Battleford school was opened in 1883 under the administration of an Anglican minister, while a second school was opened in Qu'Appelle a year later, under the Roman Catholic Oblate order. The third school was opened in High River, also in 1883, in what is now Alberta and was also administered by the Oblate order. The federal government paid for the cost of constructing the schools and assumed all costs in operating them. In that year, Public Works Minister, Hector Langevin, in justifying the costs of the schools in Parliament, stated: "If you wish to educate these children, you must separate them from their parents during the time they are being educated. If you leave them in the family, they may know how to read and write, but they remain savages, whereas separating them in the way proposed, they acquire the habits and tastes – it is to be hoped, only the good tastes – of civilized people."[33]

Langevin was not alone in his imperialistic and condescending views of the First Nations peoples. Prime Minister Sir John A. Macdonald had similar views, reflecting the position and trust of the federal government. Bob Joseph, in his book *21 Things You May Not Know About the Indian Act*[34], compiled a list of relevant quotations from MacDonald's speeches on the subject, as follows:

- "It has been strongly impressed upon myself, as head of the Department, that Indian children should be withdrawn as much as possible from parental influence, and the only way to do that would be to put them in central training industrial schools where they will acquire the habits and modes of thoughts of white men." (Speech delivered in 1879)
- "It is hoped that a system may be adopted which will have the effect of accustoming the Indians to the modes of government prevalent in the white communities surrounding them, and that it will thus tend to prepare them for earlier amalgamation with the general population of the country." (Speech delivered in 1880)
- "We acquired the North-West country in 1870. Not a life was lost, not a blow was struck, not a dollar or pound was spent on warfare. I have not hesitated to tell this House, again and again, that we could not always hope to maintain peace with the Indians, that the savage was still a savage, and that until he ceased to be savage, we were always in danger of a collision, in danger of war, in danger of an outbreak. I am only surprised that we have been able so long to maintain the peace." (Speech delivered in 1885).

Growth, Decline, and Condition of Residential Schools

As the western provinces began filling up with new settlers, the government's establishment of new residential schools moved forward at an accelerated pace with the goal of assimilating the Indigenous people into the expanding white society. By 1907, some seventy schools were in operation, and by 1930, eighty schools. Thereafter, the opening of new schools began to slow so that by 1967 the total number of schools peaked at ninety. After 1967, there was a rapid decline in the number of schools operating, with the last school closing in the late 1990s.[35]

The number of children attending the schools did not follow the pace of new school construction. Attendance at the first three industrial schools was extremely low. It was not until government officials begin forcing parents to send their children to the residential schools that enrollments increased. It is estimated that peak enrollment occurred about 1956 when just under 11,600 students were enrolled.[36] It is also estimated that, in total, 150,000 First Nations, Metis, and Inuit students attended residential and boarding schools.[37]

It was reported that many of the schools were poorly built and maintained, and there was inadequate heating and ventilation.[38] Dr. Peter Bryce, who was appointed as medical inspector to the Department of the Interior and Indian Affairs, visited thirty-five schools in 1907 and reported "appallingly unsanitary conditions, microorganism-bearing ventilation, high death rates with the almost invariable cause as tuberculosis."[39] The same year, the Hon. S.H. Blake, chair of an advisory board on Indian education, stated: "The appalling number of deaths among the younger children ... brings the Department within the unpleasant nearness to the charge of manslaughter."[40] Also in 1907, an article in *Saturday Night* magazine on the conditions of the residential schools reported: "Indian boys and girls are dying like flies.... Even war seldom shows as large a percentage of fatalities as does the education system we have imposed on our Indian wards."[41]

The government's response to the substandard operations of the residential schools was given by Duncan Campbell Scott, Deputy Superintendent General of Indian Affairs, in a letter to the British Columbia Indian Agent General in 1910: "It is readily acknowledged that Indian children lose their natural resistance to illness by habituating so closely in the residential schools, and that they die at a much higher rate than in their villages. But this alone does not justify a change in policy of this Department, which is geared towards a final solution of our Indian Problem."[42]

The Role of the Churches

For the government to succeed with its goal to assimilate the Indigenous Peoples, it needed to eradicate Indigenous languages, culture, and spiritual practices. With some missionaries already actively spreading Christianity, it seemed theologically logical, financially prudent, and politically expedient for the government to have the churches involved in operating the residential schools that were being established. In 1892, the government passed regulations that gave control over daily school administration to the Catholic, Anglican, Presbyterian, and Methodist churches. In 1925, the Methodists joined the Presbyterians and others to form the United Church in administering assigned schools.[43] At the time of the peak number of schools in operation, 60 percent were operated by the Catholic church, 25 percent by the Anglican church and the remaining 15 percent by the other churches. By 1966, the churches were no longer involved in the administration of the schools as the government took over their operations.

When the churches took over administration of the schools, whether by design or by neglect, the exact role of the schools was not established. Indeed, it appeared to be left to the administrators of each school to determine its role. It was not clear if the educational content of the residential schools was to equal the educational content of non-residential schools or whether the chief purpose of the schools was to achieve assimilation by forbidding students to use their native language and to change the students' cultural orientation and spiritual practices. For example, in 1953, J.E. Andrews, the principal of the Presbyterian school in Kenora, Ontario, wrote: "We must face realistically the fact that the only hope for the Canadian Indian is eventual assimilation into the white race." In 1957, the principal of the Anglican-operated school at Gordon's Reserve in Saskatchewan wrote that he believed that: "The goal of the residential schools was to change the philosophy of the Indian child."[44] Some thirty years earlier, in 1926, J.K. Irwin, the newly appointed principal of the same Gordon school wrote the Department of Indian Affairs for a copy of regulations on operating a residential school. Departmental secretary J. D. McLean replied: "There are no printed regulations concerning the duties and power of the principal of an Indian residential school."[45]

Coupled with the lack of direction, the residential schools were underfunded by the government for day-to-day operations that affected heating of the schools and food served to the students. In 1937, for example, the federal government was paying an average of $180 per year per student while similar provincial institutions in Manitoba were receiving about $600 per year per student. Similarly, in 1966, residential schools were spending between $694 and $1,193 a year per student while comparable child welfare institutions in Canada were spending between $3,300 and $9,855 per student per year.[46]

Student Experiences

EARLY EMOTIONAL EXPERIENCES

For the children who were forced to attend residential schools, it was a traumatic and emotional experience. At the age of five or six years, they were separated from their parents and placed in a strange environment. They had to interact with people they did not know or understand. Brothers were separated from each other, as were sisters. On arrival, students were often required to exchange the clothes they were wearing for unfamiliar school clothes. Many had their hair cut and were forced to have showers for reasons they did not understand and without their permission. They were frightened—a fright that for many lasted for their entire school experience and beyond.

During the course of their hearings, the Truth and Reconciliation Commission heard the first-hand experiences of students entering the residential school system.[47] The following is a sample of what some of the school system survivors remembered:

- William Herney, who attended the Shubenacadie school in Nova Scotia, recalled the first few days in schools being frightening and bewildering: "Within those few days, you had to learn, because otherwise you're gonna get your head knocked off. And one of the rules that you didn't break, you obey, and you were scared, you were very scared."

- Patrick Bruyere, at the Fort Alexander school in Manitoba, used to cry himself to sleep: "There was, you know, a few nights I remember that I just, you know, cried myself to sleep, I guess, because of, you know, wanting to see my mom and dad."
- Julianna Alexander, at the Kamloops school in British Columbia, said: "On my second day of school I went to speak to my brother. Did I ever get a good pounding and licking. Get over there, you can't get over there, you know, you can't talk to him."
- Timothy Henderson, who attended two different Manitoba schools, said: "Every day was, you were in constant fear that, your hope was that it wasn't you today that we're [they were] going to, that was [it was you who was] going to be the target, the victim. You know, you weren't going to have to suffer any form of humiliation."
- Shirley Waskewitch, who attended kindergarten at the Catholic school in Onion Lake, Saskatchewan, said: "I learned to fear, how to be so fearful at six years old. It was instilled in me."
- Lydia Ross, who attended the Cross Lake school in Manitoba, said: "If you cried, if you got hurt and cried, there was nobody to put their arms [sic]."
- Lorna Morgan, who attended the Presbyterian school in Kenora, Ontario, said: "I was wearing these nice little beaded moccasins that my grandma had made me to wear to school, and I was very proud of them. They were taken away from me and thrown in the garbage."

Some children experienced very traumatic experiences. Suzanne Fournier and Ernie Crey, in their book *Stolen from Our Embrace,* relate the experience of Emily Rice, who lived with her parents on a British Columbia Gulf Island. At the age of eight, Emily and her eleven-year-old sister Rose were taken by a priest by boat to a boarding school. Emily relates her experience: "I clung to Rose until Father Jackson wrenched her out of my arms.. I searched all over the boat for Rose. Finally, I climbed to the wheelhouse and opened the door and there was Father Jackson, on top of my sister. My sister's dress was pulled up and her pants were down. I was too little to know about sex, but I know now he was raping her. He cursed and came after me, picked up his big black Bible and slapped me across the face and on top of my head. I started to cry hysterically and he threw me out onto the deck. When we got to Kuper Island, my sister and I were separated."[48]

LIVING EXPERIENCES – ACCOMMODATION, FOOD, AND HEALTH

The poor construction of many of the initial industrial, and then residential, schools resulted in many hazards, including the impossibility of safe evacuation in case of fire. Martin Benson, an official with Indian Affairs, reported in 1897 that the industrial schools in Manitoba and the Northwest Territories had been "hurriedly constructed of poor materials, badly laid out, without due provision for lighting, heating and ventilation." Some seven years later, in 1904, Indian Commissioner David Laird wrote that the sites for schools on the prairies seemed "to have been selected without proper regard for either water supply or drainage." Little appeared to be done to rectify the inadequacies in building construction and maintenance over the years. For example, in 1940, R.A. Hoey, who had served as the Indian Affairs superintendent of Welfare and Training since 1936, wrote that many of the schools were "in a somewhat dilapidated condition and had become acute fire hazards."[49]

The acute fire hazard conditions identified by Hoey were very real. It was reported that over the life of the residential school system, fifty-three schools were destroyed by fire, and there were some 170 additional fires recorded, with at least forty students dying as a result. Some of these deaths were the result of exit doors being locked.[50]

Along with subpar living conditions, the students had to cope with insufficient food of poor quality. Enos Montour, who was a student at Mount Elgin school, reported that "the boys were always hungry. Grub was the beginning and end of all conversations." Similarly, Elnor Brass, who attended the File Hills Saskatchewan school, said, "dinners consisted of watery soup with no flavour, and never any meat."[51]

Theodore Fontaine writes in his book *Broken Circle* about the meals he experienced at the Fort Alexander school in Manitoba: "Our food had an overabundance of unhealthy fats, starchy food, carbohydrates, sugar and salt. A typical school breakfast was porridge. It was served almost every day. I vividly remember the bowl being about ten inches in diameter and one or two inches deep. The porridge sat in a blob in the centre of the bowl. Sometimes the porridge was warm and liquid-like, but mostly it was a cold blob. At school, Friday was a day of abstinence, so breakfast was a plate of milk made from powder. A slice of bread soaked up the milk. Lard and grease were staples. Lard was a delicacy, cut into one-and-half-inch squares about half an inch thick."[52]

One basic food for growing children that was scarce at the residential schools was milk. Many of the schools had their own herds of cattle for milk production, but often the milk was separated The skim milk was served to the students while the cream was made into butter and sold. In 1925, Inspector W. Murison reported that, at the Elkhorn Manitoba school, sufficient milk was being produced, but the students were not "getting the full benefits of the milk as 30 lbs. of butter per week was being produced and a great deal of the milk given the students is separated milk, which has not much food value."[53]

Illnesses and, in many cases, resulting deaths were much higher in the residential schools than in the general population. For example, during the period between 1941 and 1945, the residential school death rate was 4.9 times higher than the general death rate. The main causes of death were tuberculosis, influenza, pneumonia, and general lung disease.[54] The root cause of these diseases was not recorded, but it is thought to have been a weaker than normal immune system amongst students due to the poor heating and ventilation within the schools and lack of a properly balanced diet.

Proper treatment of ill students was hampered by the lack of adequate infirmary space. For example, in 1891, Indian Affairs Commissioner Hayter Reed reported that at the Battleford, Saskatchewan, school, the hospital ward was in such poor shape that ill children had to be moved to the staff sitting room. Following the influenza epidemic that killed four children at the Red Deer, Alberta, school, Principal J.S. Woodworth complained to Indian Affairs: "For sickness, conditions at the school are nothing less than criminal."[55]

EDUCATIONAL EXPERIENCES

For the most part, the residential school system did not provide education that the students could profitably use for their future vocations and careers. This shortfall was recognized within the system itself. For example, in 1923, former Regina Industrial school principal R.B. Heron reported that even though the parents generally wanted to have their children educated, they complained that their children were not kept regularly in the classroom "but were kept at work to produce revenue for the school and when they returned home they did not have enough education to enable them to transact ordinary business."[56]

The quality of the education being provided was questionable. A report on the Roman Catholic school on the Blood Reserve in Alberta noted: "The children's work was merely memory work and did not appear to be developing any deductive power, altogether too parrot-like and lacking expression." Another report, in 1932, at the Grayson, Saskatchewan, school by the school's inspector said: "The teaching as I saw it today was merely a question of memorizing and repeating a mass to the children, meaningless facts."[57] There also was confusion on the purpose of the schools, as well as lack of empathy. For example, in 1903, Brandon, Manitoba, principal T. Ferrier wrote that: "While it is very important that the Indian child should be educated, it is of more importance that he should build up a good clean character to counteract the evil tendencies of the Indian nature."[58] In addition, there was confusion on who was responsible for hiring the teachers—the churches who operated the schools or the government who paid their salaries. Because the schools were underfunded, there was difficulty in hiring qualified teachers. In 1955, 23 percent of the teachers in residential schools who were directly employed by Indian Affairs had no teacher's certificate.[59] The residential school system could not compete financially with the provincially funded school systems in hiring qualified teachers, nor in providing employment stability.

Many students found the teaching of religion and secular education by the same person confusing and overwhelming. In the case of the Catholic Church, it was even more confusing because church services were conducted in Latin, which the students did not understand, and they had to participate. Moreover, the messages the students received were scary to them. For example, they were told by the clerics that missing a Sunday mass was a mortal sin and the punishment was "burning in the fires of hell for eternity."[60] Raphael Paul, a student at the Beauval Indian Residential School, said: "Religion was so dominant in our young lives while at BIRS, many of us turned away from Catholicism later in our adult lives. We never really understood who the Christian God was."[61]

RECREATIONAL AND OTHER EXTRACURRICULAR EXPERIENCES

Recreational and other extracurricular activities were not high on the agenda at the residential schools. A national survey of both day and residential schools by Indian Affairs in 1956 concluded: "In most schools there appeared to be little or no physical education program. A number of schools had no facilities for such activities. Basement areas were obviously designed for playing areas, but they were very inadequate and were utilized for storage or for assembly purposes. A large number of school sites were not properly cleared, graded and prepared for playing purposes. Many were still in the wild state."[62]

Nonetheless, for some students, the recreational and extracurricular experiences they managed to participate in were ways to endure their negative day-to-day experiences. Noel Starblanket said that at the Qu'Appelle school: "I had some good moments, in particular in the sports side, 'cause I really enjoyed sports. I was quite athletic, and basically that's what kept me alive, that's what kept me going was the sports."[63] Similarly, at the Lestock school, Geraldine Shingoose took refuge in extracurricular activities: "One of the good things I would do to try and get out of just the abuse was to try sports. I would join track-meet, try and be, and I was quite athletic in boarding school. And I also joined the band and I played a trombone. And that was something that took me away from the school and just do, it was a relief."[64]

Hockey was a favourite sport and was played at schools on the prairies at such places as Duck Lake, Qu'Appelle, and Beauval where teams played in leagues. In some cases, residential school teams won competitive tournaments. In British Columbia, favourite sports were boxing and gymnastics. Some schools organized girls' basketball teams, while at other schools, students formed their own bands. The introduction of sport and other activities was very much dependent on teaching administrative staff taking a special interest in their students.[65]

PHYSICAL, MENTAL, AND SEXUAL ABUSE

By far, the most traumatic experiences remembered by students who attended residential and industrial schools were the physical, mental, and sexual abuses they suffered. These abuses took many forms and did not abate until the last of the schools were closed, even though government and other officials knew they were happening.

Recorded evidence and testimony of former students who participated in the Truth and Reconciliation Commission hearings are as follows:[66]

- In December 1896, in British Columbia, the Kuper Island school's acting principal gave two boys "several lashes in the presence of the pupils" for sneaking into the girls' dormitory at night.
- In 1914, a father successfully sued the Mohawk Institute principal for locking his daughter in a cell for three days on what was described as a "water diet."Boys at the Anglican school in Brocket, Alberta, were chained together as punishment for running away in 1920.
- A boy who ran away from the Anglican school in The Pas in 1925, after being severely beaten by the principal, nearly died of exposure.
- In 1934, when the principal of the Shubencadie school could not determine who stole money and chocolates from a staff member, he had the students thrashed with a seven-thronged strap and then placed on bread and water diets.
- At the Glechen, Alberta, school, a principal was accused of shackling a boy to his bed and beating him with a riding whip until his back bled. The principal admitted to having beaten the boy with the whip but denied breaking the boy's skin.
- Noel Starblanket recalled being constantly "slapped on the side of his head" at the Qu'Appelle school. One teacher struck him in the face and broke his nose.

In 1940, at the Carcross, Yukon, school, students were accused of numerous thefts. After strapping on the hands failed to have the desired effect, the principal, H.C.M. Grant, announced the next offender would "be laid across the classroom desk in the presence of the whole school, clad only in their night attire, and strapped on a different part of their anatomy than their hands." He carried through on his threat. "So severe was the strapping that the child had to be held down by the Head Matron and the Farm Instructor."[67]

Raphael Paul, in his book on his experiences at the Beauval Indian Residential School, describes this encounter: "I was going on my 3rd or 4th month at BIRS. I do not remember why I was crying. Possibly I was lonely or someone made me cry. I was on the playroom floor with my arms around my head and crying. Suddenly I was yanked up by the scuff of my neck by Brother Belanger. He placed me on his knee and wacked my behind with the palms of his large hands. I can still hear his voice to this day. 'You want to cry, well! Cry now.' Spank, spank, spank. This happened 72 years ago and I still remember the incident. All I wanted was reassurance and comfort, but the clerics knew nothing about child rearing. I learned that in order to survive one has to become hard, uncaring and devoid of emotional feelings."[68]

Besides physical abuse, students were subjected to acts that affected them mentally. For example, it was common practice to shave the heads of students who tried to run away, in front of other students. Ear pulling was another humiliating experience. But perhaps the most humiliating experiences were for those students who wet their beds. Wendy Lafond said that at the Prince Albert, Saskatchewan, school: "if we wet our beds, we were made to stand up in the corner in our pissy clothes, not allowed to change." Don Willie recalled that at the Alert Bay school: "they used to line up the bedwetters in the morning and parade them through breakfast area, pretty much to shame them."[69]

While physical and mental abuse was usually observable, sexual abuse was not. There was a determined effort by both government and church officials to "cover up" known cases for their own protection. For example, as early as 1886, Jean L'Heureux was known to have sexually abused boys in his capacity as an Indian Affairs recruiter for Roman Catholic schools in Alberta. He was forced to resign his position but was never charged. In dealing with the matter, Indian Affairs Deputy Minister Lawrence

Vankoughnet hoped, in writing, that "it would not be necessary to state the cause which led to his resignation."[70]

First- and second-year students were the most susceptible to sexual abuse. Theodore Fontaine, in his book *Broken Circle,* describes the trauma he went through as a nine-year-old student at the Fort Alexander Indian Residential School in northern Manitoba: "Every evening before we go to bed, we are in our class-room study period, and every night it happens. Four or five different boys are called into a room for a weekly ritual exercise known as menage. My name is called–can I escape? I can feel eyes on me. They know it's my time for menage—that weekly ritual, the washing of the genitals by a man in a black robe."[71] Josephine Sutherland described her moment of terror when she was cornered by a lay brother in the Fort Albany school garage: "I couldn't call for help. I couldn't. And he did awful things to me."[72] These types of abuses continued late into the twentieth century, while officials continued to dismiss them. For example, charges of sexual impropriety were made against the principal of the Gordon School in Saskatchewan. A report prepared by investigating staff was turned over to Church officials, who failed to report the case to Indian Affairs.[73] Some cases did reach the courts. Arthur Plint worked as a boy's supervisor at the Alberni residential school for two five-year periods between 1948 and 1968. In 1995, he pleaded guilty to eighteen counts of indecent assault. In sentencing him to eleven years in jail, Justice D.A. Hogarth described Plint as "a sexual terrorist."[74]

The toxic atmosphere in some of the schools created the conditions for student gangs to form and for student bullying to occur. Older or bigger boys used force or the threat of force to cause younger or smaller boys to steal or to perform sex acts. At times, older students would attack younger and smaller boys for sheer enjoyment. For example, Percy Thompson said that at the Hobbema school: "one bully used to come at me and pretend he was going to talk to me and all of sudden hit me in the belly. And of course I gag, gag and he'd laugh his head off and, you know, to see me in such a predicament."[75] Albert Elias felt that the classroom at the Anglican school in Aklavik "was the safest place to be in 'cause that's where nobody could beat me up. I dreaded recesses and lunches and after school. I dreaded those times."[76]

Indian Day Schools

The Truth and Reconciliation Commission of Canada concentrated, to a large extent, on the Indian Residential Schools. But through its investigations, the Commission also triggered an awareness of other government-sponsored schools that displayed a colonial attitude in dealing with Indigenous children and other youth. The existence of the Indian Day Schools has recently come to light due to the actions of former students who are dealing with the trauma of their school experiences.

Day schools for First Nation children were first established in what was called Upper Canada as early as the 1830s by the Methodist church with the aim of assimilation into the Anglo-Canadian society that existed at that time. Teaching included trades, crafts, and agriculture along with basic education. However, the schools proved to be unsuccessful with the result that by the 1840s, the day school program was converted into the establishment of residential boarding schools operated by the churches.[77]

The idea of day schools was resurrected by the Canadian Government in the 1920s with the establishment of a system of Indian Day Schools that were separate from the existing Indian Residential Schools. Over 700 schools were established, some on reserves and others not, which an estimated 200,000 Indigenous children attended.

Residential School Legacy

The residential school system was a failure in several ways. It failed to provide an education that the students could use in advancing their future vocations. It destroyed the bonds between children and parents that normally exist. It affected the future well-being of the students because of the abuses they suffered while attending the schools. It created mistrust amongst the students themselves. It caused confusion in the students as to their spiritual beliefs. But perhaps most disturbing was the government's continued colonial attitude toward the Indigenous Peoples, evident as late as 1969 when it proposed legislation known as the White Paper. The fundamental goals of the White Paper were: "to eliminate 'Indian' as a distinct legal status, repeal the Indian Act, void all treaties between Indigenous Peoples and Canada, and dismantle the Department of Indian Affairs. It intended to make all Indigenous Peoples 'equal' to other Canadians by removing their distinctiveness as a People and their relationship to the land, and forcing them to assimilate into mainstream society with no Aboriginal or treaty rights whatsoever."[78]

One unexpected outcome from the release of the White Paper was a strong and coordinated negative reaction by First Nations organizations. At the same time, residential school survivors started successful court actions against the government and churches for the physical and sexual abuse they had experienced at the schools. These two events caused the government to change its approach. It started to become more conciliatory in its dealings with First Nations. In addition, some of the churches began to accept their responsibility in the treatment of students under their care at the residential schools.

In 1986, the United Church was the first to make a formal apology to the First Nations for their actions and neglect in the administration of schools under their control. This was followed by apologies from the Anglican Church in 1993 and the Presbyterian Church in 1994. In 2009, Pope Benedict XVI expressed his "sorrow" to the Assembly of First Nations delegation but did not offer a formal apology. The federal government started its new approach in 1998, when it created a $350 million "community-based healing fund." In 2001, the government created the federal office called Residential Schools Resolution Canada to manage and resolve the large number of claims filed by former students. This was followed in 2003 with the launch of the National Resolution Framework, including an alternative dispute resolution process to hear former students who had been physically and sexually abused. In 2007, the Indian Residential Schools Settlement Agreement was negotiated and approved by parties and courts in nine jurisdictions. Of the 139 schools included in the settlement, 64 were Roman Catholic, 35 Anglican, 14 United Church, and the balance other or no denomination. The overall objective was reconciliation with the estimated 80,000 former students still living out of the over 150,000 enrolled since 1879.[79]

The Government of Canada's formal apology to the First Nations with respect to the Indian Residential Schools occurred in Parliament on June 11, 2008. Part of Prime Minister Harper's presentation said: "The government now recognizes that the consequences of the Indian Residential School's policy were profoundly negative and that the policy had a lasting and damaging impact on Aboriginal culture, heritage and language. While some former students have spoken positively about their experiences at residential schools, their stories are far overshadowed by tragic accounts of the emotional, physical and sexual abuse and neglect of helpless children, and their separation from powerless families and communities."[80]

In his book *Broken Circle,* Theodore Fontaine describes his thoughts and emotions related to apologies; in particular, he reflects on a ceremony in Winnipeg in 1991 when officials of the United Church made their formal apologies to the Indigenous Peoples of Canada. "At that moment, I realized that no apology could make me feel better, and I decided that I didn't need one. The moment did make me feel better about the Church itself, but watching politicians congratulating United Church officials just reinforced my belief that apologies wouldn't make *me* feel better. Only later in my healing journey did I understand that although I didn't need an apology, I began the process of forgiveness myself. Personally, the fact that I forgive, to the best of my God-assisted ability, does not mean that I forget. I still see the wandering black shadow slithering across the dormitory. I still feel the wandering and groping hands of priests, brothers, teachers, supervisors and nuns. I still feel the knuckles. I still feel the sharp-toed boot, the crack of a log on my back, the pangs of hunger and the fear of the night. While lying on my bed and praying, I seek to re-experience the manly smell of my father, the sad, kindly soft face of my mother, and the warmth of the crackling fire in our family home. My life changed forever when I was seven years old."[81]

Under the Indian Residential Schools Agreement instituted in 2007, the number of abused students began to be determined. As of January 2015, 37,951 claims for injuries resulting from physical and sexual abuse had been received by the Independent Assessment Process, established under the Agreement that investigated the claims. Some 31,000 of these claims were resolved with a payout of some $2.7 billion by the end of 2014.[82]

With respect to the Indian Day Schools, a class-action lawsuit in the amount of $15 billion by former students was filed against the government in 2009, alleging trauma that included physical and sexual abuse.[83]

On March 12, 2019, Crown-Indigenous Relations and Northern Affairs Minister Carolyn Bennett announced that the government would settle out of court for the abuses and harms perpetuated against the students. The offer that was made meant that former students would receive $10,000 each and that students who were physically and sexually abused at the schools were eligible for additional compensation of between $50,000 and $200,000, based on severity.

In announcing the proposed settlement, Minister Bennett said: "Although children who attended Indian Day Schools did leave school at the end of the day, many students experienced trauma and were subject to physical and sexual abuse at the hands of the individuals who had been entrusted with their care. Due to government policies, children were denied the opportunity to speak their language and were forced to abandon their culture. It is my sincere hope that this will be the start of a successful healing process for all of those involved."[84]

The proposed settlement was approved by the Federal Court on August 19, 2019. In addition to individual monetary payments to former students, the government offered to invest $200 million in the McLean Day School Settlement Corporation for legacy projects that support healing, wellness, education, language, culture, and commemoration.[85]

While the apologies from the government and churches were welcome and compensation offered to living residential school survivors an appropriate gesture, the root cause of the whole tragedy has not been addressed. That cause is the attitude of governments in treating certain groups of citizens as colonial subjects. For example, the closing of the residential schools only transferred the needs of children who became isolated from their parents to other government-financed programs, such as that which became known as the Sixties Scoop.

Chapter 2

Sixties Scoop - Forced Removal of Indigenous Children and Their Adoption

THE TERM "SIXTIES SCOOP" IS NOW USED TO REFER TO THE LARGE-SCALE removal of Indigenous children from their homes and their subsequent adoption by non-family members and usually non-Indigenous families. This policy by the federal and provincial governments started in the early 1960s, at the time when the residential schools were starting to be closed. As in the case of the residential schools, it was a policy the governments took with a colonial approach, without proper planning and consultation and without consideration of the consequences the forced removal and subsequent adoptions would have on the children and families involved.

Background

Prior to 1951, the federal government had full responsibility for the care and welfare of Canada's Indigenous Peoples. In the case of the First Nations, these responsibilities were undertaken with the signing of the treaties. But with underfunding, many, if not most, of the First Nation families were struggling economically, with high unemployment and substandard living conditions, particularly with respect to housing and adequate nourishment. Because of the location of many of the reserves, it was difficult, if not impossible, to establish successful agriculture enterprises and other money-generating industries. At the same time, the residential school system established by the government had achieved one of its intended purposes—children leaving schools were estranged from their families and traditional ways of life. The result was that many families lived in poverty with unstable family relations.

The federal government was aware that many First Nations families were living under duress, with high unemployment, lack of food, and high levels of alcoholism. But rather than helping the family units, it decided to target the children. And, as in the case of the residential school system, where the federal government off-loaded taking direct action by contracting with the churches to operate the schools, it contracted with the provinces to deliver First Nations child welfare services. In 1951, the government amended the Indian Act, assigning partial jurisdiction of Indigenous child welfare to the provinces.

At this time, provinces had established child welfare agencies and programs to serve their provincial populations. The contracts and resulting services between the federal government and the provinces were not uniform across Canada. For example, in the case of Manitoba, in 1966, the federal government and the government of Manitoba entered into an agreement for the existing Children's Aid Societies of central, eastern, and western Manitoba to deliver child welfare services to fourteen First Nations in southern Manitoba. Three-quarters of the bands in Manitoba were not covered by the arrangement. In Saskatchewan, the province established a separate agency called the Adopt Indian Metis (AIM) Program to facilitate the adoption of Indigenous children.

The transfer of responsibility for Indigenous children from the federal government to the provinces was a difficult one for the provinces. A former minister of social services in the Province of Saskatchewan has indicated that the programs were underfunded in comparison to the need to care for Indigenous children living in dysfunctional homes. In addition, the First Nations communities declined to work with the provincial authorities because they wanted to maintain the position that servicing the Indigenous populations was a federal and not a provincial responsibility.[86]

Implementation

Having taken on the responsibility of Indigenous child welfare, provincial governments concluded that the fastest and easiest way to deal with the conditions being experienced by Indigenous families was to remove the children from their homes and have them adopted. This was carried out in an arbitrary way, without the parents' permission or the permission of the band councils. Most of the children who were taken from their homes were placed in non-Indigenous families throughout Canada and sometimes in the United States and Europe. The social workers who assessed the family homes and placed the children for adoption had little or no training and little experience in cross-cultural situations arising from the arbitrary placement of Indigenous children in "white" homes, where the way of life and cultural approaches were vastly different and where the adopted children had no contact with their siblings and relatives. The potential for successful adoption of Indigenous children by non-Indigenous families was extremely variable. Marie Adams, in her book *Our Son a Stranger*, narrates her family's unsuccessful experience and the difficult experiences of five other families in raising Indigenous children and the trauma that the adopted children endured.[87]

The removal of Indigenous children from their families and their subsequent adoption was most intensive from the late 1950s to the 1980s. For example, in British Columbia in 1951, there were twenty-nine Indigenous children under provincial care. By 1964, the number had grown to 1,466. In Manitoba, between 1971 and 1981 approximately 3,400 Indigenous children were adopted. According to Indigenous and Northern Affairs Canada, some 11,130 children were adopted between 1960 and 1990. However, according to other sources, the number of adoptions was closer to 20,000.[88]

Probably the most aggressive effort to remove children from their homes and have them adopted occurred in Saskatchewan under the AIM Program. This program proactively searched for adoptee families, claiming to be a part of the solution to such things as the "rise of illegitimate births and marriage breakdowns" among Indian and Metis people. It carried out a marketing campaign through radio, television, and newspaper advertising, even showing photographs of the children that were up for adoption. The program also promised fast adoptions with completion of the process within as few as ten weeks. The program went so far as to create a "Salesperson of the Year" award to recognize the number of children made wards of the province and eligible for adoption by a program staff member.[89]

Reports and Policy Changes

In 1983, Patrick Johnston, a program director at the Canadian Council on Social Development, prepared a report titled *Native Children and the Child Welfare System.* His research showed that Aboriginal children were being disproportionately taken into the child welfare system. He estimated that, across Canada, Aboriginal children were four and a half times more likely than non-Aboriginal children to be in the care of child welfare authorities. Another study, in 1980, by the Canadian Council on Social Development, found 78 percent of status First Nations children who were adopted were placed in non-Indigenous families.[90]

In 1985, Associate Chief Judge Edwin Kimelman released a report commissioned by the Government of Manitoba on the status of the Indigenous adoption program under way in that province. He found the system to be flawed in that it discriminated against Indigenous parents, particularly mothers, with respect to their Indian status, marital status, and place of residency. The report noted that some 25 percent of Manitoba adoptees were placed outside the province. Judge Kimelman concluded that the treatment of children perpetuated by the system was "cultural genocide."[91]

Following these and other reports, the Manitoba government brought in changes to how the programs were to be administered. The first change was that before children could be placed with non-Indigenous families, priority for adoption was given to extended families and then to other Indigenous families. The second change gave local communities the power to administer child and family services according to provincial and territorial legislation.

The Impact

Raven Sinclair, an associate professor at the University of Regina and a member of Gordon First Nation, published an article in 2007 titled *Identity Lost and Found: Lessons from the Sixties Scoop* in which she said:

> "At the same time as we may be alarmed by the statistics, it is important to recognize that the Sixties Scoop was not a specific welfare program or policy. It names one segment of a larger period in Aboriginal child welfare history where, because questionable apprehensions and adoption figured prominently, a label was applied. The Sixties Scoop has evolved as a descriptor that is now applied to the whole of the Aboriginal child welfare era, simplistically defined here as roughly the time from the waning of the residential schools to the mid-1980s period of child welfare devolution and closing of the last Indian residential schools...
>
> The white social worker, following on the heels of the missionary, the priest and the Indian agent, was convinced that the only hope for the salvation of the Indian people lay in the removal of their children."[92]

The residential school system broke down ties within families in which family members would traditionally take care of one another in times of need. The widespread adoption of Indigenous children compounded this breakdown with the dispersal of adopted children amongst adopting families, usually long distances away from their homes. Wayne Christian, a former Spallumcheen band chief, relates how he and his nine younger siblings were separated through the adoption process. When he was seventeen years old, he returned to his band community to find that his birth mother had become an alcoholic in trying to deal with the trauma of losing her children. At the same time, one of Christian's brothers also returned home after an unhappy life with his foster parents. Christian describes what transpired: "We tried to be a family, and I tried to connect with my brother to what I found to be strong and good about our culture, but it was lost to him." One morning Christian found his brother dead by suicide.[93]

The overpopulation of Canada's jails, shelters, and youth detention centres with Indigenous youth is well-known. A 1990 survey of aboriginal prisoners in the Prince Albert Federal Penitentiary found that over 95 per cent came from either a group home or a foster home.[94] Similarly, Jerry Adams, a social worker for the Vancouver's Urban Native Youth Association, estimates that half to three-quarters of all the habituated native street kids he worked with "are graduates of the B.C. foster care system or runaways from adoptions that didn't work out."[95]

The impact and subsequent trauma of the Sixties Scoop experienced by those affected lingered for many years. The following are the stories of two adoptees.

Betty Ann Adam's Story

Betty Ann Adam, an adoptee and a reporter for the Saskatoon *Star Phoenix*, in an article published by the *Readers Digest* in 2017, said: "I'm three years old, I'm wearing a plaid dress that I don't usually wear. It's too small. A policeman and a lady are in the room and they're really nice to me. My mother's arms are tight around me, she's crying and pleading. I don't know why they are taking me away from her. I'm in a police car. It's a hot summer's day and the seat is burning my legs. The woman puts me on her lap. Next I'm in an airplane looking down on tiny cars on the road. Finally, I'm at the farm where, without knowing why, I'm living a new life. I was part of the Sixties Scoop.

"My birth mother, Mary Jane Adam, attended Holy Angels Indian Residential School in Fort Chipewyan, Alta. She left school in her teens, but never returned to the reserve to live. She was twenty-two and single when I was born in Uranium City, a fly-in mining town in the northwest corner of Saskatchewan, eighty-five kilometres west of our home reserve of Fond du Lac. My sister Esther was born two years after me. In the early

1960s, few in Canadian society had less power than an unmarried Indian mother with kids. Social workers took Esther when she was three months old. My mother got to keep me for almost another year, but in 1962, they pried me away from her arms. The memory of that moment has never faded, but as an adult it's my mother's pain that haunts me."[96]

Colleen Cardinal's Story

Colleen Cardinal, a Sixties Scoop adoptee, has written her and her family's life experiences in a first-hand and compelling book titled *Raised Somewhere Else.* [97] Colleen and her two sisters were adopted by a non-Indigenous family while she was still a baby. Colleen was born in 1972, sister Gina was born in 1970, and sister Dakota was born in 1971. Colleen's mother, Dolly Ester Cardinal, attended Blue Quills Residential School in Alberta from 1962 to 1966. She died early in life, at the age of forty-nine. Colleen states that after she reconnected with her father, Richard Cardinal, when she was an adult, he told her that there was turmoil in the family with alcohol consumption and physical abuse. Colleen's research found that adoption documents showed there was "neglect, unfit conditions and severe alcohol usage" in the family home.

In 1975, Colleen and her sisters were placed in a non-Indigenous foster home in a rural area some twenty-five kilometres outside of Sault Ste. Marie, Ontario. Physical abuse by the foster father started with spankings and beatings for such reasons as poor grades at school, not cleaning the floors properly, not cleaning her room properly, and forgetting homework. During the beatings, the foster mother took a passive view and did not intervene.

When Colleen was about ten years old, she and her sisters wanted to flee their abusive home and decided to visit the Children's Aid Society in Sault Ste. Marie for assistance in finding a new home. The social worker they dealt with was uncooperative and drove them back to their foster home, where their foster father beat them and grounded them for their efforts in exposing their situation. Some five years later, the three girls left their adoptive home to escape the physical and sexual violence they were experiencing and went their separate ways. Colleen lived with a number of friends in the Sault Ste. Marie area and, at the age of sixteen, moved to Edmonton. But before leaving Sault Ste. Marie, Colleen's sister Gina reported to police their foster father's sexual abuse against them. Charges were subsequently laid, and the father was found guilty of gross indecency and sexual interference and ordered to pay restitution to two sisters in the amount of $15,000 each. He was also required to serve time in a North Bay mental health facility.

In 1996, Colleen decided to return to Sault Ste. Marie, taking three of her four children with her. She enrolled in the Native Community Worker Addictions Counsellor Diploma Program at Sault College, graduating in 2002. After graduation, she became employed at the Women in Crisis centre.

In May 2011, Colleen decided to move to Ottawa, where she worked with friends, writing and speaking about her experiences. She gradually began a new life and helped form an organization called The National Indigenous Survivors of Child Welfare Network. She went on to filmmaking and speaking to groups about her experience and those of others who were caught up in the Indian Residential School system and the Sixties Scoop.

On a visit back to Alberta, Colleen visited her mother's gravesite at the Oniheikiskowapowin Reserve. Here she acknowledged to herself her sometimes disappointing thoughts about her mother's behaviour but was able to understand her mother's life as a youth and her experience as a residential school student, with its residual effects.

Colleen wrote in her book: "The 60s Scoop was an aggressive tool for assimilation and cultural genocide through the Canadian welfare system. Now, I have people say to me, 'Your life turned out better because you were raised in an adoptive home by white people,' but I beg to differ. Sure, I had opportunities like sports and travel, but by and large I was robbed of a life that I will never get back. My biological parents were both fluent Cree speakers, and I had a very large extended family of aunts, uncles and cousins all over Saddle Lake/Goodfish Lake and surrounding area that I cannot re-integrate into. I lost the protection, familiarity and socialization opportunities of knowing my own people and by 'people' I mean Nehiyawak (Plains Cree) within my own territory. That *cannot* be replaced.

I grew up feeling homesick and unsettled in the adoptive household, ready to run away at any sign of danger." [98]

Lawsuits, Apologies, and Financial Restitution

Starting in the 1990s, individual and group class-action suits by adoptees were beginning to be filed against governments for the physical, emotional, and sexual abuse they experienced as Sixties Scoop adoptees.

In June 2015, the Province of Manitoba issued an apology for the Sixties Scoop and announced that this history would be included in school curricula.[99]

In February 2017, Ontario Superior Court Judge Edward Belobaba ruled in favour of Sixties Scoop victims, finding that the federal government did not take adequate steps to protect the cultural identity of on-reserve children taken away from their homes.[100]

In October 2017, the federal government announced a proposed settlement of $800 million with First Nations and Inuit Sixties Scoop victims. Non-status and Metis victims were not included in this proposal.[101]

Saskatchewan Premier Scott Moe, on January 7, 2019, issued an official apology on the Saskatchewan's government's role in the Sixties Scoop. As noted previously, Saskatchewan was one of the most aggressive jurisdictions in implementing and promoting the adoption process through its AIM program. In his apology to survivors and their families present at the ceremony, Moe said: "We are sorry for the pain and sadness you experienced, for the loss of culture and language, and for the loss of family contact."[102] The premier promised increased government support in areas of education, health and culture, but no monetary compensation was offered.

Chapter 3
Unwed Mothers and Their Babies and Duplessis Orphans

INTERNAL COLONIALISM CAN TAKE DIFFERENT FORMS THAT AFFECT A variety of groups. One such group consists of unwed mothers and their babies who were born immediately following World War II. In this case, as in others where colonial attitudes prevailed, the state predetermined what was best for a certain vulnerable segment of the population. Here, governments, along with churches and other organizations, decreed that a child born to an unwed mother was better off being raised in a foster home or institution than by its mother. In many of these forced interventions, both the mother and the child were negatively affected for years.

Unwed Mothers and Their Babies – Unwanted by Society

The treatment of unwed mothers and their babies in Canada and elsewhere has its roots in European class attitudes. For example, England's colonial attitude prevailed, not only within government, but also amongst upper-class families. Offspring deemed to be a potential disgrace to the family were sent to live in one of England's colonies or former colonies such as Canada and Australia. The family member, so exiled, and who was usually a male, received a living allowance or remittance to stay away and not return to England. The term "remittance man" was coined to refer to someone that the family felt would cast a bad shadow on their social standing.

This same colonial attitude prevailed in Canada but under a different form. A large number of unwed mothers and their newborns were deemed to be a disgrace by family members, the churches, and the Canadian federal and provincial governments. In the years from 1945 to 1973, an estimated 350,000 unwed mothers were persuaded, coerced, or forced to give up their babies for adoption in an attempt by those in control to preserve their public image, without consideration of the trauma the young mothers, and in later life, their children, would experience.[103]

Background

In the immediate years following the Second World War, Canadian society was in a state of flux, as was the case in other countries that had participated such as Australia, New Zealand, the United Kingdom, and the United States. The war caused upheavals within families, uncertainty about the future, and a change of lifestyle from what had existed previously. Women, for example, had come to know greater independence, after having experienced work outside the home in factories that manufactured war equipment and materials. Men were returning home to an uncertain future. There was a loosening of the previously tightly controlled family structure. However, social attitudes of governments and organizations such as the churches did not change and remained rigid with respect to child-raising outside of the traditional family structure. Children born outside a marriage were classified as illegitimate and the mother as a second-class citizen.

The Process and the Outcomes

As in the case of the Sixties Scoop, the federal government provided the finances, and the provinces, with the assistance of some churches and civil-society organizations, implemented a plan to separate newborns from their mothers. The process was subtle and secretive, carried out with the assistance of family members who wanted to distance themselves from the expectant mother. The laying of guilt for the perceived lack of regard for social norms was used extensively and persuasively as a motivator to have the young mothers give up their babies for adoption.

Until the Standing Senate Committee on Social Affairs, Science and Technology report titled "The Shame is Ours," published in July 2018,[104] there was very little public information on the adoption of babies of unmarried mothers in post-war Canada. In its research, the Committee heard testimony from mothers who gave up their child for adoption, adoptees, child welfare agencies, family reunification organizations, religious organizations, and other interested parties.

Generally, unmarried pregnant women were placed in maternity homes, which were mainly established and operated by religious organizations. Federal funding paid for their operating costs as well as for adoption services. The provinces, and in some cases municipalities, were responsible for the oversight of the physical operation of the homes.

According to the testimony presented to the Senate Committee, young, scared mothers were sent to the maternity homes by family, social workers, or clergy. There they endured verbal and emotional abuse and, in some cases, were forced to use fictitious surnames. During their stay in the maternity homes, they were discouraged and even prevented from contacting their families and the babies' fathers. At the end of their pregnancies, the mothers were transferred to hospitals for labour and delivery. Some of the mothers who testified to the Senate Committee reported that they were separated from the married mothers at the hospital and left alone. Others reported they were mistreated during delivery, and they were either under- or over-medicated. Some mothers indicated that they were not allowed to see their baby or have any further contact with the child after birth.

Government-paid social workers, assigned to work with the young mothers-to-be, provided little or no information on the options available to them. Some of the mothers reported that they were coerced into what they were told would be best for the child, meaning giving up the baby for adoption. Social workers provided the legal forms for signature without the mother having any legal representation to explain the meaning of the documents. Once signed, the mothers were usually not given a copy of the documents.

Family pressure contributed to the adoption of babies born to unwed mothers. Jennifer Charles recalls that in 1968, at age eighteen, when she told her parents she was pregnant, her father told her that if she did not give her baby up for adoption, he would disown her. After seeking advice from the Children's Aid Society, her social worker advised her to give up the child for adoption because it needed a father as well as a mother.[105]

While mothers who had given up their babies felt the anguish in the years that followed, the adopted children also lived with an emptiness, especially when their adoptive parents were less than accommodating and nourishing. Adoptees who testified before the Senate Committee talked about not knowing who they were and where they came from. Some tried to search for documents that might provide information on their origins but found that they were either not available or not accessible. In some provinces, where adoption documents exist, they may be only semi-open, such that either the birth parent or child can prevent the disclosure of information.

The outcome of the treatment of the young mothers who gave up their babies for adoption was devastating for many. The Senate Committee was advised that mothers were told not to speak of their experiences to anyone. No counselling was provided: mothers had to deal with the emotional consequences on their own. According to the testimony provided at the hearings, some 80 percent of the women who were subjected to mistreatment in the maternity homes and hospitals suffered depression. About 20 percent of abused mothers attempted suicide. It was reported that an estimated 30 percent of the mothers were so traumatized by their experiences that they refrained from having babies later in life.

The Search for Identity and Recognition

There has been, in recent years, an organized interest by individuals and organizations to trace adoptions both from the mother's and the adoptee's sides. For example, one fifty-year-old mother was reunited with her long-lost daughter while working as a volunteer with an organization called Parent Finders, based in Ottawa. In her case, there had been ongoing communication between the birth mother, the adoptee mother, and the adoptee herself.[106] In another case, Valerie Andrews, who was forced to give up her son when she was seventeen, reunited with him thirty-one years later. She now works with an organization called Origins Canada that has been requesting, since 2013, that the federal government hold an inquiry on the forced adoptions.[107] Another organization, called the Canadian Council of Natural Mothers, is working to expose the negative treatment in adoptive situations.[108]

In an effort to gain information on the services, treatment, and experiences at the maternity homes, the Senate Committee invited representatives of the Catholic, United, Anglican, and Presbyterian churches and the Salvation Army to testify before the committee. Only the United Church of Canada attended. It expressed regret for its role in forcing unmarried mothers to surrender their babies for adoption. The Salvation Army provided a written submission that stated it regrets the "harsh attitudes of the time." [109]

The Senate Committee received information that there was a movement in Australia, where forced adoptions also occurred, to have the Australian government offer an apology to all those affected by the post-war treatment of unwed mothers and their babies. There has been no indication from the Canadian government that it intends to issue an apology for its similar role. The majority of the churches involved appear to have taken a "hands-off attitude," claiming that these events occurred under different circumstances and attitudes. In the meantime, individual and class-action suits against the government are being contemplated.

Duplessis Orphans

The Duplessis orphans were children living in Quebec in the 1940s and 1950s who were wrongly certified as mentally ill by the Duplessis government for its financial gain as well as that of the institutions caring for the children. The children were orphans, abandoned children, children deemed socially vulnerable, children living in poverty, and children born out of wedlock. They were originally housed in institutions labelled as orphanages.

During this period, the Quebec government provided only limited social services directly to its citizens; the bulk of the services were provided by the Roman Catholic Church on a fee-for-services basis. The federal government provided the Quebec government subsidies for operating hospitals and orphanages. The federal support was $1.25 a day for orphans, but $2.75 a day for psychiatric patients. The Quebec government with the assistance of cooperating physicians had the children diagnosed as mentally incompetent and placed in psychiatric hospitals, mostly operated by religious organizations affiliated with the Roman Catholic Church.[110]

It is estimated some 22,000 children were involved in the scheme of labelling children as mentally incompetent. In a study conducted in 1999, researchers Leo-Paul Lauzon and Martin Poirier concluded that: "religious groups received $70 million in subsidies (in 1999 dollars) by claiming the children as mentally deficient, while the government saved $37 million simply by having one of its orphanages re-designated from an educational institution to a psychiatric hospital."[111]

Some survivors of the psychiatric hospitals spoke in later years about the harsh treatment and sexual abuse they suffered at the hands of medical personnel and other staff. Some said they were subjected to lobotomies, electric shock, and straitjackets. In a study carried out at one of the hospitals, it was found that middle-aged Duplessis Orphans had more physical and mental impairments than the study control group. The study also found the orphans were less likely to be married or to have a healthy social life, with 80 percent reporting they had suffered traumatic experience between the ages of seven and eighteen. Over 50 percent said they had suffered physical, mental, or sexual abuse, and about 78 percent reported difficulty functioning socially or emotionally in their adult lives.[112]

Some of the approximate 3,000 survivors in the 1990s began a campaign to obtain apologies from the Quebec government, the College of Physicians of Quebec, and the Roman Catholic Church. They were unsuccessful with the College of Physicians and the Church, but on March 4, 1999, the Bouchard government issued an apology and offered the group $3 million with no individual compensation. The surviving Duplessis Orphans declined the offer and continued their lobbying. On June 30, 2001, the Landry government offered an apology and compensation that amounted to approximately $25,000 per person for the 1,500 people qualified for compensation. After some unsuccessful negotiations, the group accepted the offer that included a "fault-free" clause and an agreement to drop legal action against the Church, which declined to offer any apologies for its alleged role in mistreating the children.[113]

Chapter 4

World War I and World War II Internments

ALL NON-INDIGENOUS CANADIANS ORIGINATE FROM WORLDWIDE EMIGRATION. During the war years, many senior politicians and civil servants were from Great Britain, a colonizing country. Because of this, some believed that immigrants from other countries should be thought of as "foreigners" and treated with suspicion, including those who were naturalized Canadians or born in Canada. During World Wars I and II, many Canadians who, or those whose ancestors, had come from countries at war with Great Britain were deemed to be "enemy aliens" to be watched and controlled. This suspicion of loyalty even applied to members of labour unions and those affiliated with pacifist organizations.

World War I Internments

With the outbreak of the World War I, Canada, whose foreign policy was still under British control, became a participant, even though the war was thousands of kilometres away. At that time, it was decidedly a "British" colony, notwithstanding the mixed population or immigration base from countries around the world.

On August 22, 1914, the Canadian parliament passed the War Measures Act, giving the government broad powers with respect to matters related to the country's security. Within a few months, the government established twenty-four internment camps across the country and interned 8,579 men, women, and children as enemy aliens. In addition, it established a registry of some 80,000 other Canadians who were required to report to authorities on a monthly basis. It was reported that of the 8,579 interned, 5,954 were labelled as being of Austro-Hungarian origin, but were, in fact, Ukrainians, Croats, Ruthenians, Slovak, and Czechs. Of the remaining internees, 2,009 were of German origin; 205 were Turks, and 99 were of Bulgarian origin. The vast majority of the Austro-Hungarian-labelled internees were of Ukrainian origin. According to Sir William Otter, the Canadian military officer in charge of all of the internment camps, 3,138 detainees were labelled prisoners of war—meaning that they had been captured or were enemy reserve soldiers. The rest were civilians.[114]

The War Measures Act and the Wartime Elections Act

The War Measures Act gave the government sweeping powers without providing any means of questioning or debating its actions. The Act allowed the cabinet to bypass the House of Commons and the Senate and to govern by Order-in-Council. Some specific examples of the authority it had are:

- People could be arrested, detained, and deported without specific charges and without trial or legal counsel.
- Transportation, trade, and manufacturing were controlled.
- Private property could be seized.
- Publications, writings, photographs, and communications could be censored and suppressed.

In a case before the Supreme Court of Canada in 1943, the Court confirmed the validity of the Act and also concluded that the Act could be amended by regulation, from time to time by Order-in-Council.[115]

The War Measures Act provided the government with the authority to label Canadians and others living in Canada whose origins were from Austro-Hungary, Germany, and the Ottoman Empire as "enemy aliens," even though some were Canadian-born or naturalized British subjects.

The Wartime Elections Act was passed in September 1917. It disenfranchised those who came to Canada after March 1902. One result of the

Act was that it eliminated the ability of any persons negatively affected by it from voting against the government in the following general elections. It also laid the seed for permanent resentment, as recorded in the *Daily British Whig* newspaper: "It is quite probable that if the Wartime Elections Act becomes law the alleged 'foreigners' and hitherto 'naturalized' Canadians will bear their reproach meekly, but they will have sown in their hearts the seeds of a bitterness that can never be extirpated. The man whose honour has been mistrusted, and who has also been singled out for national humiliation, will remember it and sooner or later it will have to be atoned for."[116]

Who Were the "Enemy Aliens"?

Starting in the late 1800s and into the 1900s, the Canadian government promoted immigration to Canada as part of its national policy.[117] To populate western Canada with peoples of agricultural background, it sent agents to Eastern Europe, promising free land in exchange for the promise to till and develop the land and infrastructure. Immigration was not limited to agriculture alone: men with experience in the mining, construction, and lumber industries were welcomed as well as those who were willing to work as general labourers. Between 1891 and 1914, it is estimated that some 170,000 immigrants from Ukraine came to Canada.[118] Some obtained land for farming while others worked in resource industries or as general labourers. The same opportunities were offered to other nationalities from central and eastern Europe, including substantial numbers from Germany.

In the years immediately preceding World War I, the Canadian economy was in a downturn, with considerable unemployment. As a result, there was growing antagonism and prejudice against the new Canadians, especially those who maintained customs from their native lands and who lived and socialized together. Open bigotry was displayed toward the new immigrants. Some citizens felt that they were of inferior stock as compared to those of British ancestry. With the outbreak of the World War I, there was little sympathy for the new Canadians subjected to internment, and some encouragement was given to the government for its internment policies. The feeling was that this would free up jobs for the non-immigrant population.

Officially defined, enemy aliens were those living in Canada who had come from countries that were at war with Great Britain. These included Austro-Hungary, Germany, Bulgaria, and the Ottoman Empire. In the case of Austro-Hungary, it included Ukrainians, Poles, and peoples of other countries that were, at that time, occupied by the Austro-Hungarian Empire and who, for the most part, had no particular loyalty to the empire. Many were, in fact, hostile to the occupying force.

There were two categories of enemy aliens—those who were forced to live in internment camps and those who were allowed to live independently but had to register and report to a government official on a monthly basis and had restrictions on their freedom of speech, movement, and association. Among the enemy aliens, the criterion used by government officials to identify those who were to be subject to internment appeared simply to be unemployment.

The Internment Camps

There were officially twenty-four internment camps set up across Canada, with the first ones established in 1914 and the last closed in 1920. The camps, for the most part, were situated in remote locations. They housed German and other prisoners of war and Canadians deemed to be enemy aliens. Most of the barracks and other facilities at the camps were recycled buildings: among them were an iron foundry, an armoury, an exhibition building, a government building, a park building, and some railway cars. The largest camps were located at: Vernon, BC; Banff National Park (Castle Mountain), Alberta; Brandon, Manitoba; Kapuskasing and Petawawa, Ontario; and Spirit Lake, Quebec.

Most of the internees were single, but some were married and had children. While wives and their children were not forced to be interned, some did so to be close to their husbands and, in some cases, because they had no means of surviving otherwise. The camps in Vernon and Spirit Lake accepted women and children.[119]

The camps were all secure, usually fenced by barbed wire and patrolled by armed militia. Each one had a camp commander. Sir William D. Otter was in overall charge of all the camps. Otter's military service dated back to 1885, when he led a militia attack against a community of Cree First Nations at Cut Knife, in what is now the Province of Saskatchewan.[120]

INTERNMENT CAMP OPERATIONS

Many of the internees were required to do manual labour, especially at the remote camps where building roads, clearing bush, and building parks were government priorities. In some instances, such as at Kapuskasing and Spirit Lake, the internees were engaged in establishing experimental agricultural farms in heavily-treed areas.

The appropriateness and even the legality of forcing the internees into manual labour was questioned, but it was never definitively resolved, except by passing an Order-in-Council that was never tested in court. The incentive to require the internees to do manual labour from the government's point of view was strong. Many of the internees were there mainly because they were unemployed and thus, in the government's view, more likely to become subversive. There was a desire at some of the camps to do road work, construct bridges, and other similar projects using low-cost labourers. To try to overcome any doubt about legal issues, the government passed Order-in-Council 2721, clause 10, which stated: "Canadian militia would oversee the maintenance of the enemy aliens as prisoners of war, who would perform work as required."[121] The 1907 Hague Convention, an international set of protocols for wartime, protected prisoners of war from forced labour. The Convention allowed prisoners of war, except officers, to work at various tasks, as long as "the projects had no connection with the war effort, the labour was not excessive and the men were paid at a rate equivalent to that of a soldier." The British government urged Canada not to abuse subject nationalities of the Austro-Hungarian Empire who were, in fact, friendly to the British Army and hostile to Austro-Hungary.[122]

There was some segregation of internees within the camps. Prisoners of war were generally separated from the enemy alien internees, and there was some segregation on a class and ethnicity basis. Generally, and depending on the camp, conditions were less than satisfactory, and there was unrest amongst the internees. For example, in May 1916 some 1,200 internees rioted at the Kapuskasing camp. It was recorded that in all the camps, 107 internees died in captivity, six were shot dead while attempting to escape, while others died in camp from disease, work injuries, and suicide.[123] In many cases, the dead were buried in unmarked graves in poorly kept cemeteries. Those who survived remembered those who perished. Many years after the camps were closed, a former Kapuskasing prisoner, who returned to pay his respects, said: "Here, the men who cleared the forests lay forgotten by the world as if they were made by another God. But I had not forgotten them. As I walk back into town, I remembered what we all promised each other in camp. We were going to tell the world about how we were tortured, and it would become part of history."[124]

In wartime, there are agreements amongst the belligerent countries that prisoner-of-war camps can be examined by a neutral country to ensure that prisoners are treated properly. In World War I, before the United States joined the war in 1917, it was tasked with examining the prisoner-of-war camps in Canada. In November 1916, Gebhard Willrich, US Consul stationed in Quebec City, was asked to report on the conditions of the Spirit Lake camp. Willrich reported, based on his interviews, that the internees lived in shacks without heat. They were deprived of food, and he had heard of beatings, confinement, insults, and neglect. He also reported that: "The man charged with police authority at this camp.... had exercised his authority in a rather brutal way, under the mistaken notion, that these prisoners were criminals rather than unfortunate under the circumstance. Petty annoyance, loss of small liberties, even physical punishment had thus resulted solely to gratify the petty officer's brutal instincts."[125] In December 1916, Willrich, in a report to the United States Secretary of State, wrote: "The prisoners in Canadian Internment Camps came to the Dominion as peaceful emigrants and the great majority of them at least have been good, law-abiding residents since their arrival, doing their bit to further the development of its great resources. In other words, these men now held as prisoners, as a class, are good, sturdy, inoffensive men, able and willing to work, most of them desirous of becoming Canadian citizens. The idea, therefore, of a treatment of such men as quasi-criminals seems contrary to the very best interests of the Dominion... There is no doubt in my mind, that at the present moment, the great majority of the prisoners at Sprit Lake could safely be returned to their homes and families, and that such return would be more profitable to Canada in the end than their retention in the camps as unwilling workers or strikers."[126]

Several of the camps were kept open until 1920, two years after the war ended. No official explanation was given, but it was speculated they were kept open to continue utilizing the inexpensive labour provided by the internees.

PERSONAL ACCOUNTS OF INTERNMENTS

There were few personal accounts written by internees of their camp experiences. There was even a reluctance to tell family members about the experiences of internment because of shame and stigma and the fear that there could be repercussions from government officials. Perhaps internees thought that once an enemy alien, always an enemy alien. At the same time, the government destroyed much of the archival material it had on hand.

Some documentation left by internees and family members attests to their experiences:

- Katie Domytryk, then nine years old, wrote to her father, who had been arrested in Edmonton in March 1916, interned initially in the Lethbridge camp, then moved over 2,500 kilometres east to the Spirit Lake camp in Quebec: "My dear father: We haven't nothing to eat and they do not want to give us no wood. My mother has to go four times to get something to eat… This shack is no good, my mother is going down town every day and I have to go with her and I don't go to school at winter. It is cold in that shack. We your small children kiss your hands my dear father. Goodbye my dear father. Come home right away."[127]
- Nick Olynyk, prisoner No. 98 at the Castle Mountain Camp in Banff, wrote his wife: "As you know yourself there are men running away from here every day because the conditions here are very poor, so that we cannot go on much longer; we are not getting enough to eat. We are hungry as dogs. They are sending us out to work, as they don't believe us, and we are very weak."[128]

- Mary Bayrak was born at the Spirit Lake camp. She was the daughter of Nikolai and Felicia Hancharuk, who were interned at Spirit Lake at the time of her birth. Mary wrote about her recollections: "My parents spent their honeymoon in the camp.... Edward (my brother) and I were listening to Dad talking to someone. We heard the adults talking. The government was saying that those interned weren't Canadian citizens. They took my parents up north to Spirit Lake. The men were working logging and did something that they shouldn't have. The soldiers used to punish them by making them carry water pails taken from one place to another and digging holes. Edward and I thought it was a terrible thing to be in a camp. We thought it was for doing something wrong."[129]

- Jerry Bayrak was the son of Mary Bayrak and grandson of Nikolai and Felicia Hancharuk, all internees at Spirit Lake camp. Jerry wrote: "There was an epidemic of tuberculosis at the Spirit Lake camp. They built a huge circular incinerator out of rocks to burn clothing and bedding in. There were three women interned in my family who got tuberculosis. My Great-grandmother Anna, my grandmother Felicia and my mother Mary. My grandma died in her thirties as a result of TB. I didn't get a chance to know her.... Family never talked about it, friends never talked about it. So, yes I'm really pleased that all of this is coming into the open."[130]

- Philip Yasnowsky was an internee at the Stanley Barracks Toronto and then Kapuskasing. He wrote: "One day, Barrack No. 4 was ordered to vacate. Its inmates were assigned to other barracks. We were told that No. 4 was to get 100 new occupants. ... We were appalled by the appearance of these men. Their faces were yellowed and emaciated, they all looked haggard - old and young without exception. It was a frightful sight. We tried to find out from where they were rounded up. Their speech was hard to understand, for they all spoke with difficulty – some with tears. They complained that they had not yet a morsel of food in their mouth that day...After supper, we listened to their stories about their hard lot. They had been interned at the camp near Petawawa. There were 600 of them in all. All were forced to do hard labour. When the Feast of Annunciation rolled around, the internees at the camp asked for a day off from work to observe the holy day. But it was not to be. No one paid attention to their request. The commander of the camp responded with, 'to hell with your holy day' and the internees were all ordered to go to work that day. The next day, no one turned up for work. The camp officials summoned them, one by one, and demanded an explanation of why they refused to go to work. They all had the same answer: 'You did not capture me on the battlefield. I came to Canada not to fight a war, but to earn a living and to enrich this country with my labours.... At the end of the questioning, one of them declared on behalf of the entire group – because you are forcing us to work on a holy day, we are not going back to work ever.'"[131] The position taken by the internees in Barrack 4 not to do further work escalated throughout the camp when all camp internees decided not to work. A special commission undertook an examination of the situation at the camp with the result that all of the internees there were allowed to leave.[132]

– Christine Witiuk related the story of when authorities came to pick up her father and uncle Emile Litowski at their home late at night: "Here is a story from World War I. The two men knocked on the door and walked in and they asked dad's name. The younger brother was there. His name was Emile...they asked his name, then asked for his last name, and they told my dad and my uncle that they had to come with them. They are taking them because they expect war in Europe and they want them to defend Ukraine because they are Ukrainian. They were going to take them both that same night. And they started to cry, my dad and mother, because it's winter time, it's cold, and Dad says that he can't leave Mother alone with the children because she won't survive. And those men said that it is not their problem. The problem is to pick them up and take them to defend their own country. Then finally, Dad and Uncle got them to wait to morning...they'll go in the morning. They didn't want to go because this was already dark. Those men went with lanterns. But Dad did not go in the morning. My Uncle Emile went alone and they took him and they never came for Dad, never picked Dad up. Before Mother died I asked her what happened to Emile. This is exactly what she said. Dad didn't go and they never picked him up, Emile went like they said. There was a rumour that they were taking them as spies. They were putting them in internment camps. So that's probably it. Emile never came home. So where they took him, we don't know."[133]

- Mary Manko Haskett was six years old when she was interned with her parents, her brother, and two sisters at the Spirit Lake camp. She recalled living in a cold and drafty building and that her two-year-old sister, Nellie, died from an infection in her lungs. "They put two pennies on her eyes and made a cross," said Fran Haskett, Mary's daughter.[134] Mary remembered her mother crying and crying. It was only when she was an adult that she was finally able to tell her story of her family's forced confinement to her own children. Her children did not believe her at first because the story was not in the history books, and Spirit Lake could not be found on the map.[135] Mary Manko Haskett was the last known survivor of the Spirit Lake internment camp. She was born in 1908 in Montreal. Her parents emigrated from western Ukraine, then occupied by the Austro-Hungarian Empire. She spent fourteen months at the camp – from April 1915 to June 1916. Once an adult, she served as the honorary chair of the National Redress Council of the Ukrainian Canadian Civil Liberties Association. Mary Manko Haskett died in Mississauga, Ont. on July 14, 2007, at the age of ninety-eight.[136]

In addition to the Canadians labelled as enemy aliens and forced to live in the internment camps, there were thousands of others who were allowed to live independently, but, in many cases, lost their jobs and means of earning a living. A letter published in the *Calgary Daily Herald* on February 29, 1917, and signed by twelve women read: "We, the undersigned, Ukrainian and Austrian women, wish to bring before the notice of the women of Calgary that we came to this country to make Canada our future home. We are not spies. Thousands of our men are fighting under the British and Russian flags. We have been discharged from work because we are considered aliens, but we are loyal to Canada. What are we to do if we cannot get work? Are we to starve or are we driven to a life of vice? Will the women of Calgary speak for us?"[137]

Ukrainian Canadians in the Canadian Armed Forces

One of the ironies of the government's policy in classifying Ukrainian Canadians and other immigrants as enemy aliens was that many enlisted in the Canadian army and fought against Germany and Austro-Hungary in Europe. In the case of Ukrainian Canadians, the exact numbers are not known, but H.A. Mackie, MP, Edmonton East, recognized their contribution when he told Prime Minister Robert Borden in October 1918 that Ukrainians had enlisted in greater proportion than other immigrant groups: "To estimate the number of Ukrainians who have enlisted...would be very hard as they were enlisting in various battalions from the Atlantic to the Pacific, but it is safe to say that... these people, per population, gave a larger percentage of men than certain races [British Canadians] in Canada have, after having enjoyed the privileges of British citizenship for a period of a century or more." [138]

A Ukrainian Canadian from western Canada, Corporal Filip Konowal, was awarded a Victoria Cross for bravery while fighting with the Canadian Army at the Battle of Hill 70 in August 1917.[139]

Ukrainian Canadian Restitution Act

Once the impact of the War Measures Act and subsequent internment and registration policies became recognized, publicized, and understood, the Ukrainian Canadian community began organizing a campaign to approach the government to recognize the wrongdoing inflicted on Ukrainian Canadians and others during World War I. The Ukrainian Canadian Civil Liberties Association (UCCLA) under its first chairman, John B. Gregorovich, and others, such as Lubomyr Luciuk, took the lead in mounting a campaign to have the government recognize the injustices made and to offer some form of restitution. The task was helped by Conservative MP Inky Mark when he submitted private member's Bill C-331. As a result, the Ukrainian Canadian Restitution Act was passed and became law on November 25, 2005. Negotiations between the government and UCCLA, the Ukrainian Canadian Congress and the Ukrainian Canadian Foundation of Taras Shevchenko resulted in the establishment of the Endowment Council of the Canadian First World War Internment

Recognition Fund. The Council was officially established on May 9, 2008. The Endowment Council represented all ethnocultural communities affected by the internment operations. A fund of $10 million was established, dedicated to supporting commemorative and educational projects that highlighted the internment years.

There was no monetary restitution to individuals under the Restitution Act, even though the personal belongings and other properties of internees were confiscated by the government and not returned after the end of the internment operations. Also, in some cases, the $0.25 per day payment for work at the camps that was promised to the internees was never paid.[140]

World War II Internments

There were three instances of the internment of Canadian citizens during World War II – of Japanese Canadians, of Italian Canadians, and of labour leaders. In all cases, no actual evidence of sabotage or genuine threat to Canada's war effort or security was discovered. All three instances are examples of internal colonialism undertaken by the federal government and based on misguided assumptions and prejudices, not on factual conditions.

Internment of Japanese Canadians

The attack on the US naval base at Pearl Harbor in the Hawaiian Islands by Japan on December 7, 1941, precipitated a tragic upheaval of Japanese Canadians living along the west coast of British Columbia. It has been estimated that starting in early 1942, over 22,000 Japanese Canadians were forcefully evacuated from their homes and moved inland in the name of "national security."[141] The decision by the Canadian government was made without any evidence that Japanese Canadians living along the west coast of the province created a real or potential risk to the security of Canada. The move by the government was an arbitrary one, carried out under the War Measures Act, without any opportunity for the people affected to defend themselves in a court of law. The decision to relocate and, in some cases, to jail Japanese Canadian citizens in internment camps was based solely on their ethnicity, with racist overtones. This act demonstrated a colonial approach and prejudice, both at the federal and provincial government levels.

BACKGROUND

Early Immigration

Manzo Nagano, a nineteen-year-old sailor, is recorded as the first Japanese person to immigrate to Canada. He began working in the fisheries industry in 1877. Although prior to 1868, it was illegal for Japanese citizens to leave their country, there was a pent-up desire amongst young Japanese, especially men, to find economic opportunities beyond Japan. Many wanted to settle in the United States, but some were not permitted to land and were diverted to Canada. By 1887, regular steamships travelled between Japan and British Columbia carrying immigrants.[142] Early immigrants worked in the fisheries industry, either fishing or working in canneries. Later, they sought employment in the forestry and mining industries. As the young Japanese males became established in Canada, they sought wives from Japan, sometimes by sending a picture of themselves to family members back home who would use the picture to find a suitable and willing wife.[143]

Early Life in British Columbia

Unlike some of the other provinces in Canada where the early populations were a mixture of different backgrounds and cultures, such as English, French, Scottish, Irish and American, the vast majority of British Columbians were of English stock and had direct ties to England. Some of these people, especially in leadership positions, carried forward colonial prejudices against minorities. As a result, Japanese immigrants "faced legislated racism, unfair living and working conditions and a population that wanted them gone."[144]

Most of the early immigrants secured low-paying jobs both in the Vancouver area and in towns along the coast, and they often lived in substandard housing. Women found it difficult to find work as most factories hired men only. Due to language barriers, there were limited opportunities to work in the service industries. Notwithstanding the difficulties the early immigrants encountered, they worked hard at earning a living and with the goal of accumulating wealth, so they could start their own businesses, especially in the fisheries industry.[145]

Growth, Success, and Setback

Japanese immigration to British Columbia continued to grow in the late 1800s and early 1900s, particularly after the United States began prohibiting access to mainland America through Hawaii. For example, in 1906 some 2,040 Japanese citizens entered Canada. After the United States decision in 1907 to curtail immigration from Japan, that number increased to over 7,000. The Japanese immigrants also became more aggressive in their search for employment and business opportunities. By 1919, 3,267 Japanese immigrants held fishing licences and 50 percent of the total licences issued that year were issued to Japanese fishermen.[146]

The success of the Japanese immigrants in the fishing and then farming industries began to draw resentment from the general British Columbia population. This attitude was exacerbated by the growing Chinese population in the province who had come to Canada to work on the construction of railways in the province. There was a growing feeling that the increasing Asian population was undermining the province's way of life. There was some decline in the resentment of Japanese immigrants during World War I when a number of the Japanese Canadians enlisted in the Armed Forces and fought in Europe. This change in attitude was, however, short-lived as the returning non-Japanese servicemen found that their previous positions of employment were occupied by the new immigrants, resulting in their need to find different employment.[147]

As the number of Japanese immigrants grew, they—as did immigrants from other countries—lived close to one another. They established their own community organizations, places of worship, and in some instances, their own schools. These developments led to greater distrust by the general public and provincial authorities. As a consequence, the provincial government enacted a number of laws and ordinances forbidding workers of Japanese origin from joining labour unions, working in underground mining, working in forestry on Crown lands, and working in provincially licensed professions, as well as forcing some of the fishermen to give up their fishing licences.[148] These government actions affected all residents of Japanese descent, even if they were Canadian citizens through naturalization or by birth. At the same time, anti-Asian organizations such as the Asiatic Exclusion League were formed to stop any further immigration to British Columbia and to advocate the return of Chinese and Japanese immigrants to their home countries. Unfortunately for the Japanese Canadians living in Canada, actions in the 1930s by the Government of Japan encouraged further mistrust by the general population. These included Japan's withdrawal from the League of Nations in 1934, refusal to follow the Second London Naval Treaty in 1936, and alliance with Germany with the Anti-Comintern Pact.[149]

In the years immediately before World War II, there were approximately 29,000 persons of Japanese descent who lived in British Columbia. It is estimated that approximately 80 percent of them were Canadian nationals but without the right to vote.[150] There were continuing accusations that the Japanese Canadians could not be trusted and that their prime loyalty was to Japan, not Canada. No incident or event to justify this attitude was ever presented publicly. With the outbreak of World War II in Europe in September 1939, Japanese Canadians joined Canada's war efforts by purchasing war bonds, sending canned salmon to England, and volunteering to enlist in the Canadian Forces.[151]

Prior to its bombing raids on Pearl Harbor, Japan had attacked a number of countries in Southeast Asia. This triggered a reaction by the federal government against Japanese Canadians living in British Columbia. Compulsory registration was imposed on all males over the age of sixteen in March 1941, and the Japanese Canadian community was placed under police surveillance. Six weeks prior to the Japanese attack on Pearl Harbor, Canada sent 2,000 troops to Hong Kong, a British colony at that time, in case of attack by Japan.[152]

CANADA AT WAR WITH JAPAN AND GOVERNMENT DECISIONS

Immediately following Japan's attack on Pearl Harbor on December 7, 1941, discrimination and action against Japanese Canadians increased. In the following days, 1,200 Japanese Canadian-owned fishing boats were impounded by the police. On January 4, 1942, the federal government passed an order that required the removal of male Japanese nationals between the ages of eighteen to forty-five years from a designated protected area of a hundred miles inland from the Pacific coast. For the duration of the war, the federal government also banned Japanese Canadians from fishing and from using shortwave radios. It controlled the sale of gasoline and dynamite to Japanese Canadians.[153]

On February 24 and 25, 1942, the federal government widened its actions. It required the removal of all persons of Japanese origin from any protected area in Canada. This included all Japanese Canadians, whether naturalized Canadian citizens or citizens born in Canada. In some cases, there was even deportation to Japan. The laws also provided for the confiscation of all property with all Japanese Canadians designated as enemy aliens. Individuals affected had no legal recourse as Canadian citizens in protecting their rights and freedoms or their property. While there were some officials in government and elsewhere that felt that the actions taken against the Japanese Canadians were unwarranted, the federal government held firm in its decisions.[154]

RELOCATION TO WORK CAMPS, ROAD WORK, AND INTERNMENT CAMPS

The relocation of men, women, and children from their homes and places of work was a traumatic experience for approximately 22,000 Japanese Canadians. Of these, some 14,000 were born in Canada. Widespread relocation began on February 24, 1942 with an Order-in-Council passed under the Defence of Canada Regulations under the War Measures Act. The regulations gave the federal government the power to intern all "persons of Japanese racial origin" from a one-hundred-mile-wide strip along the Pacific coast that was deemed "protected."[155]

The first wave of those relocated were mostly Japanese nationals who were sent to work on roads under construction in interior British Columbia and to tend sugar beet farms in Alberta. The second wave consisted of Japanese Canadians who were sent to road camps and as labourers to farm camps and orchards. In both cases, men were sent out alone, leaving their families behind. When the time came for the rest of the family to move, the wives had the burden of closing down their places of residence and of moving their children with them.

Most of those relocated were initially housed and processed at the Hastings Park facility in Vancouver. Hastings Park was the home of the Pacific National Exhibition. The main buildings used for accommodation and processing the internees were livestock stables. These living spaces were unsanitary with remnants from their previous use of housing livestock remaining. The buildings were cold and drafty, and there was little privacy. Bedding material consisted of bags stuffed with straw. The conditions were so bad that the Canadian Red Cross began supplying food and other materials to the internees.[156] Mary Ohara, a young internee at that time, recorded her experiences: "We were herded like animals. I was careful not to step on the excrement that had dried on the concrete. I felt sick from the stench so I climbed as quickly as I could onto the top bunk for some air. From there I saw the hundreds of other families moving into the stalls. Overhead were swallows. They had their homes in the rafters and were swooping down quite close to the bunks."[157]

In the relocation process, adults were restricted to bringing 150 pounds of belongings, while children were allowed 75 pounds each. All remaining property, including houses, appliances, cars and clothing, were left in the care of the Custodian of Enemy Alien Property. One relocating mother, Mary Haraga, wrote: "We took with us only the bare essentials we could carry: – cooking pots, rice bowls, chopsticks, bedding and clothes and some food – rice, soya sauce, sugar, salt, vinegar, and canned goods." Mary Ohara, aged twelve at the time of relocation, wrote: "I wanted to take my one and only doll but my mother said there was only space for necessities such as dishes, pots, pans and bedding so I hid her in the corner of the attic and promised to come back for her soon. It was not to be."[158]

SEIZURE OF PROPERTY

The property of the Japanese Canadians subjected to evacuation orders was taken over by the Custodian of Enemy Alien Property. This included community-owned property, such as churches, temples, language schools, and hospitals. It was originally thought that the confiscated property would eventually be returned to its owners. However, in January 1943, the government, through an Order-in-Council, ordered that all of the property taken over by the custodian be sold. This included homes, businesses, cars, trucks, boats, farms, equipment, furniture, and all the other goods not taken by the internees at the time of their relocation. Many of the properties were sold at vastly reduced prices, and in some instances, there was looting from empty homes and businesses before sales occurred.

The proceeds from the sale of the confiscated properties were kept by the Custodian of Enemy Alien Property, and the monies raised were placed in accounts under the former property owners' names. The internees could withdraw $100 per month from their account, but the money had to be used to cover their living expenses while they were being kept in confinement.[159]

LIVING CONDITIONS

While most men were sent to work camps or detention centres, women and children were sent to old abandoned mining towns and hastily built camps that, in some cases, were initially comprised only of tents. Living conditions were harsh, especially during the winter months. In many cases, there was no running water, and toilets were outdoors. The buildings were drafty, and wood-burning space heaters were used for heating purposes. Akira Horil, an internee, writes of his experience: "Drinking water, trucked in by the barrel, had to be paid for. In the wintertime, snow was melted for drinking. Water for washing and bathing was pumped from the muddy Fraser River, filtered and stored in holding tanks nearby. We hauled it on our backs in five-gallon cans. There was no electricity. Wood was logged in the nearby mountains, trucked to homes, cut, chopped, and stacked by the shack."[160] Mary Ohara, along with her mother and four siblings, arrived at Lemon Creek internment camp in the BC interior where they were housed in a 14 x 24 foot uninsulated shack that they shared with another family. She writes: "We (the two families) alternated between having our meals in the kitchen and in the bedroom where we used the beds as dining tables. The first winter was unbelievable. We were always cold. We had to scrape the ice off the walls and ceiling in our cabin before the pot-bellied stove was lit and puddles formed on the floor. But we were better off than the families who were still living in canvas tents because not enough shacks were built."[161]

The provincial government did not provide education for the interned children as they did for other children in the province. However, the federal government eventually agreed to pay for teachers up to grade eight. The internees, over time, with the help of the BC Security Commission, constructed their own schools and equipped them with homemade desks. In some cases, church organizations became involved in teaching, and in some communities, high schools were established.[162]

PROTESTING AND PUNISHMENT

As the relocation process developed and the draconian actions intensified, some began to question the legality of what was happening. Others began reacting to promises made, but not kept. Takeo Nakano was one such person. He kept a diary and published his memories in a book titled *Within the Barbed Wire Fence.*[163] Nakano was born in Japan, the second son of a rice farmer, with very little chance that he would inherit the family farm. Nakano wrote: "I had, however, this uncle who owned a farm in Canada, and he used to correspond with my father. One day my father asked if I wanted to emigrate to Canada. My uncle was prepared to sponsor me. Though only fourteen at the time, I leapt at the chance. During the next two years, I often stood on the shore of the inland sea Suo Nada, dreaming of farmlands as vast as the ocean. Someday I would own such lands in faraway Canada, not a tiny farm like the farms in Japan." In 1920, Nakano immigrated to Canada, and as planned, worked at his uncle's berry farm near Hammond, BC. But, due to an economic downturn, he had to leave the farm and move to Woodfibre to work at the British Columbia Pulp and Paper Company. In 1930, he returned to Japan for a short visit, got married, and returned to Canada and Woodfibre. After Pearl Harbor and by mid-January 1942, discussions began in the town about the possibility of evacuation. Nakano writes: "At that time it was said that if the Issei (Japanese-born) men aged eighteen to forty-five went to road camps, then the Issei men over forty-five, the Issei women and children, and all Nisei (Canadian-born of Japanese descent) would be allowed to remain where they were. We Issei men accordingly received an order to depart on March 16."[164]

On March 16, Nakano and others were transferred by ferry from Woodfibre to Vancouver and were taken to Hastings Park. On the next day, Nakano, with a group of some 150 men, boarded a train to Yellowhead, which was nearly five hundred miles east of Vancouver. At Yellowhead, the men were taken to their new home – a string of twelve freight boxcars. After three weeks at Yellowhead, Nakano was transferred to another road camp at Desoigne, in the same area, where he worked on a bridge. Again, home consisted of boxcars until canvas tent-houses were erected.

In July 1942, with the work completed at Desoigne, Nakano was told by the Security Commission that he was to be transferred to Greenwood where his wife and child were. However, on the day of his departure, he was told that instead of Greenwood, he was being sent to the Slocan camp. On arrival at Slocan, Nakano and six others, who were told they were to be transferred to Greenwood, met with the Security Commission representative and asked to be sent to Greenwood. Their request was denied. The men then decided to protest and not report to work for the following four days. As a consequence, Nakano and the other men were taken to the immigration building jail in Vancouver and subsequently were sent to a prisoner-of-war camp at Angler, located north of Lake Superior in northern Ontario.

Nakano's train at Angler was met by soldiers who escorted the men to their barracks, which were located within a double-fenced area. There were about eight hundred prisoners at the camp, some of whom were bitter about the way they were being treated by the Canadian government and expressed the hope that Japan would win the war. In 1943, the Federal Department of Labour, due to the labour shortage resulting from the war, began offering employment to qualified detainees at the camp. In November, 1943, about fifteen months after he arrived at the camp, Nakano applied to leave the camp. He was successful and was offered a job with Canada Packers in Toronto, which he accepted, arriving in Toronto on November 17, 1943. His only obligation with respect to his internment was to report to the RCMP once every month. After the war ended, Nakano's wife and daughter were able to join him in Toronto. In December 1948, he and his wife became Canadian citizens.

DEPORTATION

In the spring of 1945, the Canadian government gave notice to all persons of Japanese origin, whether Canadian-born or not, that it was inviting applications for voluntary deportation to Japan. Since almost all of the Japanese Canadian population was now living outside the province of British Columbia, this was a racist, economics-driven intent to discourage their return to that province. All of their homes and businesses had either been sold off or destroyed. Notwithstanding that the war was ending and that there was no longer an excuse to take action against the Japanese Canadians on grounds of disloyalty, they were still not allowed to live in the BC coastal areas. Mary Ohara wrote: "In the spring of 1945 we got word that everyone over sixteen years of age must choose exile to Japan or re-settlement east of the Rockies. If we refused to leave BC, it would be seen as evidence of disloyalty. It was frightening to have an RCMP officer come to the door to ask, have you made up your mind? Are you going to Japan? If we answered yes, the government would pay for the transportation and we would be allowed to stay in BC until our departure. If we said no, our income would be cut off and we would have to leave BC anyway."[165]

Mary Ohara's mother decided to move to Japan. In June 1946, Mary, her mother, and four siblings boarded the *General M.C. Meigs*. She wrote: "My mother wanted to see her own mother. Furthermore, she was a penniless widow with five teenage children, one of whom was mentally challenged. She found the prospect of going east, to yet another unknown and hostile place, too frightening. We had to abide by our mother's decision."[166] In 1949, the government finally lifted the restriction against Japanese Canadians to live along the west coast of British Columbia. Mary Ohara subsequently, on her own initiative, returned to her native country, Canada, in 1954.

GOVERNMENT ACTION AND ITS CONSEQUENCES

Why did the government take the action it did with respect to the internment of Japanese Canadians, using the War Measures Act as its legal vehicle? Researcher Ann Sunahara examined government documents written in the 1940s regarding the actions taken by the government. Her findings indicate that the federal cabinet's decisions to expel Japanese Canadians were based, not on national security, but on the politics of racism. She writes: "The government's documents demonstrate that each Order-in-Council under the War Measures Act that affected Japanese- Canadians – uprooting, confinement, dispossession, deportation and dispersal – was motivated by political considerations rooted in racist traditions, accepted, and indeed encouraged, by persons within the government of the day. At no point in the entire seven years of their exile were Japanese Canadians ever a threat to national security."[167]

The 1941 Canadian census reported that there were 22,096 people of Japanese ancestry living in British Columbia, mostly in coastal towns. Of that number, 12,426 were male and 9,670 female. The consequences of the government's policies respecting the removal and relocation of Japanese Canadians from their homes was drastic. In 1947, six years after the policies were put in place, only 6,776 Japanese Canadians remained in British Columbia. About double that number, 13,782, had moved to other parts of Canada. Almost four thousand (3,964) had been deported to Japan, 66 percent of whom were Canadian citizens.[168]

GOVERNMENT ACKNOWLEDGEMENT OF WRONGDOING, APOLOGY, AND REDRESS

In 1977, the Japanese Canadian community began to organize a petition to the federal government asking it to acknowledge the wrongdoing that had been inflicted upon its people. Some eleven years later, with the support of other Canadian ethnic organizations and individuals, the federal government offered an acknowledgement, apology, and an offer of redress. On September 22, 1988, Prime Minister Brian Mulroney stated: "The Government of Canada acknowledges that the treatment of Japanese Canadians during and after World War II was unjust and violated the principles of human rights as they are understood today."[169] The redress portion of the apology consisted of a grant of $21,000 per living individual who suffered under the wartime policies, $12 million for educational and cultural projects and $24 million to establish a Canadian Race Relations Foundation.[170]

Internment of Italian Canadians

On June 10, 1940, Italy joined Germany in World War II and declared war on the United Kingdom. Within days, the Canadian Minister of Justice signed an order that resulted in labelling 31,000 Italian Canadians as enemy aliens. With the right to normal proceedings and trial suspended, between 1940 and 1943 some 600 to 700 Italian Canadian men were arrested and sent to internment camps. They were deemed to be potentially dangerous enemy aliens without actual evidence of any crimes being committed.[171] The interned men were sent to two main camps, Petawawa, Ontario, and Minto, New Brunswick. The Italian Canadians deemed as enemy aliens but not sent to internment camps were required to register with authorities every month.

In 1990, at a National Congress of Italian Canadians held in Toronto, former prime minister Brian Mulroney offered an apology to the attendees: "On behalf of the government and the people of Canada, I offer a full and unqualified apology for the wrongs done to our fellow Canadians of Italian origin during World War II."[172] In 2010, an Act: "To recognize the injustice that was done to persons of Italian origin through their enemy alien designation and to provide for restitution and promote education on Italian Canadian history" was passed by the House of Commons but never became law.[173] In June 2019, Prime Minister Justin Trudeau stated at an Italian Canadian function that his government would be making an apology for the treatment of Italian Canadians during World War II.[174]

Internment of Labour Leaders

Following the First World War, there was high unemployment in Canada, which resulted in labour unrest. One outcome was the Winnipeg General Strike that occurred between May 15 and June 25, 1919. It is estimated that some 30,000 workers in Winnipeg left their jobs. The strikers included private-enterprise factory workers and public-sector employees. The strike was terminated when the federal government intervened. Some of the union leaders were arrested.[175]

The Winnipeg strike laid the seed for increased union development in Canada, especially since there was a further slowdown of economic activity through the subsequent general recession of the late 1920s and 1930s. At the same time, some of the unemployed workers became attracted to the Communist movement as a solution to high unemployment and low wages.

On August 29, 1939, the governments of Germany and the Soviet Union signed a non-aggression pact that provided a guarantee of non-belligerence between the two countries. On September 1, 1939, Germany invaded Poland. Two days later, Great Britain declared war on Germany; Canada followed suit on September 10. Technically, Germany and the Soviet Union were not allied, but were, at the same time, considered to be working together. The Canadian government took the position that Communist sympathizers in Canada should be viewed with suspicion.

On January 11, 1940, the Canadian government passed legislation under the War Measures Act that gave it the power to arrest and detain people without having to lay charges or hold any trial. In June 1940, an Order-in-Council was passed, which declared the Communist Party illegal in Canada. Immediately thereafter, police began arresting and detaining individuals who they thought were members of the Communist Party. Caught in the roundup were leaders of labour organizations that were not affiliated with the Communist Party. Arrests and detentions were based on suspicion only, without evidence of any illegal activity. An estimated 250 people were interned in camps established in Kananaskis, Alberta; Petawawa, Ontario; and Hull, Quebec. Most were released in 1942 after Germany invaded the Soviet Union, and the Soviets became allied with the west in fighting Germany.[176]

Jehovah's Witness Denomination Banned

In 1940, one year after Canada entered World War II, the Jehovah's Witness denomination in Canada was banned under the War Measures Act. The ban was placed primarily because the denomination's adherents were conscientious objectors to military service. The ban continued until 1943, during which time some children were expelled from school or placed in foster homes, some members were jailed, and others were sent to work camps. No evidence was ever presented that members of the denomination were ever a threat to national security.[177]

Chapter 5

Forced Relocation - Quebec Inuit, the Nunavut Ahiarmiut, and the Manitoba Sayisi Dene

THE CANADIAN GOVERNMENT PRACTISED INTERNAL COLONIALISM through the relocation of Canadian Indigenous people. Three such events occurred around 1950: the relocation of Inuit who lived in northern Quebec, the relocation of Ahiarmiut who livedg in what is now Nunavut, and the relocation of the Sayisi Dene in northern Manitoba.

The Inuit People

The present-day Inuit people began to occupy northern Canada about 1,000 years ago. They came from Alaska in a series of small migrations and reached the west coast of Greenland about 1300. The Inuit came after the Tuniit, who had occupied the region previously but were unable to survive.[178] The traditional Inuit territory lies north of the "tree line" which itself varies across the Canadian north. It is estimated that there are about 65,000 Inuit living in Canada. Prior to contact by non-Inuit, the Inuit lived exclusively off the land, sustaining themselves on water animals, land animals, and birds.

The Inuit have a very strong attachment to the land and to the environment, both physically and emotionally. Anthropologist Robert Williamson described the Inuit as having strong family commitments and loyalties and that the relocation to a distant place for an extended period of time would be very difficult for them. The hardship could involve a sense of isolation, feelings of loneliness, a loss of meaning of life, and a powerful need to be at home and see kin.[179] Melanie McGrath, in her book *The Long Exile,* described Inuit characteristics as restrained and self-contained. According to her, the typical Inuit was cheerful, calm and patient in adversity, immune to irritation, sulking, or to the hostility of others. He/she took life as it came, recognized its limits, and accepted its various outcomes.[180]

Initially, the only non-Inuit people that the Inuit met were the Royal Canadian Mounted Police who projected power, control, and singular authority to which the Inuit were not accustomed. Their feeling of inferiority was perpetuated when the fur-trading companies established themselves in the north. The Inuit became dependent upon the trading companies who provided credit to the trappers, obligating them to pay it off with furs, thus establishing a master-servant type of relationship. Rosemarie Kuptana, president of the Inuit Tapirisat of Canada, described the Inuit feeling toward non-Inuit during the 1950s as follows: "There is an Inuk word that characterizes the feeling that whites inspire on Inuit. The word is *illira,* which is not easy to translate. It is a kind of fear, a blend of awe and intimidation, the feeling you have about a person whose behaviour you can neither control nor predict, but who is perhaps going to be dangerous. It is a feeling you have when you are in a room full of important strangers whose language you cannot understand, the feeling inspired by the trader, the missionary, the policeman and white strangers who were so obviously powerful, upon whom the Inuit were so acutely dependent and who told people what to do and believe, but who were not often disposed to listen to what Inuit wanted to do and believe."[181]

Hugh Brody described the Inuit relations with persons of authority that helps to explain how the Inuit and whites differed in their interpretations of acceptance and consent. "In the course of two or more decades of dealing with the whites, Inuit came to have expectations and attitudes strongly influenced by the *illira* they felt. They did not expect to be able to state their own opinions and criticisms of what southerners were doing, they tended to accept the decisions of traders and missionaries to avoid all possible confrontation. This meant they were inclined to smile and look cheerful whenever they had dealings with whites, it also meant that they did what they were asked to do, even in reality, something they thought wrong or foolish."[182]

Quebec Inuit Relocation

The relocation of Inuit families from northern Quebec to new homes in the High Arctic took place in 1953 and 1955. The designated camps were well north of the Arctic Circle, in areas that were uninhabited except by military personnel and police officers.

In August 1953, seven Inuit families from Inukjuak, Quebec, (then known as Port Harrison) and three Inuit families from Pond Inlet on Baffin Island were relocated to Craig Harbour on Ellesmere Island and Resolute Bay on Cornwallis Island. Of the ten families, six went to Craig Harbour and the other four went to Resolute Bay. There were fifty-four persons involved in the relocation.

The second relocation occurred in 1955 when four families from Inukjuak and two families from Pond Inlet were relocated to Craig Harbour. There were ninety-two persons involved in both relocations. The Inukjuat families were unaware they would be joined by the families from Pond Inlet, who were complete strangers to them. The government had planned to establish a third community at Cape Hershel on the east side of Ellesmere Island but were unable to do so because ships could not get through due to ice conditions.

Relocation and Living Conditions

According to the report *The High Arctic Relocation* prepared by the Royal Commission on Aboriginal Peoples, the relocation plan approved by the deputy minister was: "little more than a concept – a very general description of what was to be done and for what purpose. The detail would be worked out as the plan was implemented. This would mean that a large amount of discretion would be left to those implementing the decision." Also, according to the report, "action to implement the relocation decision began in the second week of April 1953. The action taken would result in the modification of the plan; the failure to obtain genuine consent from the Inukjuak relocatees; the forced separation of the relocatees into different groups; the relocatees arriving in the High Arctic lacking essential equipment and supplies; and instructions to the RCMP that would make the coercion inherent in the relocation a daily reality for the relocatees."[183]

There was a breakdown in communications between government officials and the Inuit. For example, the government told them they were being relocated so they would have a better life, but they were not told exactly how that would happen and what would be better. The Inuit were promised by the RCMP in charge of the move that they could return home if they did not like their new location, but this was never offered. The Inuit were not told until they arrived in the High Arctic that they would be split up into different communities. The Inukjuak Inuit were not told that the Pond Inlet Inuit would be joining them and for what reason. And the Inuit from Inukjuak were not told that they would be living in complete darkness for some two months of the year. The Pond Inlet Inuit understood that they would be compensated for helping the southern Inuit acclimatize to the harsher northern conditions, but they were never paid.

The weather and environment at Craig Harbour and Resolute Bay were considerably different than at Inukjuak. Winter temperatures were some 12 to 16 degrees F colder, the winters were longer and darker, the terrain more rugged and treeless, and the availability of game for food was uncertain. The Inukjuak Inuit found living conditions difficult and much harder than they had expected. From the government's point of view, the relocation was an experiment, as noted in the High Arctic Relocation Report. Only a small number of Inuit were being sent north "to see whether they could adjust successfully and with a view to increasing the size of the communities if the first relocations were successful."[184]

In treating the relocation as an experiment, the government must have considered that there was a possibility that the outcome could be catastrophic, especially for the Inukjuak Inuit. One reason for the relocation was to force the Inuit to live exclusively off the land, as they did prior to non-Inuit occupation of the north. However, the ability to live off the land was not established prior to the relocation. This situation was recognized by the High Arctic Relocation Report: "The inherent riskiness of the project was not discussed with the Inuit. They were simply assured that there was abundant game in the High Arctic and that they would have a better life. This adds further to the conclusion that the Inuit did not give free and informed consent to the relocation."[185] The report goes on to say: "The belief of the relocatees that they were betrayed and abandoned by their government was the direct consequence of not disclosing the true character of the relocation to the Inuit. The relocatees had no idea that the relocation could fundamentally alter their way of life. They thought instead that they were going to a place where they would have a better life. The objective of requiring greater reliance on hunting and less reliance on the trade store was inherently coercive."[186]

Stories of Relocatees

During its hearings in 1993, The Royal Commission on Aboriginal Peoples invited Inuit who had been subject to the relocation to relate their experiences. Some twenty-nine persons responded. Most spoke in Inuktitut with their testimony translated into English. The following is the testimony provided by Minnie Allakariallak and Samwillie Elijasialak, the first two to testify. Their stories were told through a translator and are recorded in the Commission's report.

MINNIE ALLAKARIALLAK

The translator's account of Minnie's story is as follows:

> "Minnie Allakariallak was born in the Inukjuak area in 1916. She relocated to Resolute Bay in 1955. She reported that her family was going to go on the original trip in 1953 but her father did not want to move to another place. Her husband Johnny was worried about being left behind but also did not want to leave her father behind. As a result, they did not go on the original trip.

"They had been approached in 1953 by the RCMP using Josie Nowra as the interpreter and were told that they had to leave. 'You have to leave to another community. The government wants you to move.' When Qallunaat (white person) spoke, 'We were afraid of them.'

"In the Inukjuak-Povungnituk area there was firewood and plenty of food. Codfish was the regular diet in the summertime and even in the wintertime the people would fish for cod. There was plenty of seal meat, fish and birds, 'so we were not worried.' They told us, 'you are hungry and you would have to move where there is lots of game.'

"Her family had not been thinking of moving anywhere else. They felt obligated by the requests of the police and imagined a place where there was plenty of vegetation. But Resolute Bay was a desert, just gravel. When they arrived, they had to use tents to stay warm and it was very cold. Later her husband got wood from the dump to build a house. It was hard for her because she had polio and found walking very difficult. There was nothing at Resolute Bay to heat the houses, no lumber, no oil, no anything to warm themselves.

"She remembers that they were told: 'you will be home maybe in a year or two,' but after two years she remembered her husband asking when they would be going back. They had no way of knowing. No one told them.

"The people were suffering. They wanted to see their families again in Inukjuak. There were no government services. The people had to do everything for themselves. There was an Air Force base there but people from the base were not allowed to come down and help in any way.

"They believed strongly in God. Her husband was a lay reader. They asked God to help them.

"In the Inukjuak area, all men were equipped and the food the hunters obtained was shared equally. The people had the joy of life and absolutely no care in the world, with very good family relations, even with those who were not directly related by blood. They were happy in the original homeland. They were shocked when they were told that they should leave the place. We [sic] were not clear on the reasons. It was a great strain to part company with relations. At Inukjuak, they did not want for anything. They were secure and happy. The place they went to was so desolate. People were devastated.

"Her oldest daughter, Sarah, was married to Simeonie Amagoalik. They went with the first group. Sarah was pregnant when they went because Minnie and her husband had planned to be part of the first group but they did not go. Her husband was very worried about the security of relatives going to the High Arctic in the first group but Minnie's father would not agree to go with the first group.

"The police were quite insistent that they should agree to relocate to an area that had plenty of wildlife. The police did not tell them about the disadvantages – the extended periods of darkness, the lack of vegetation. 'They only told us there were lots of seals and lots of walrus.'

"They were never told they would be joined in Resolute by people from Pond Inlet. The people from Pond Inlet were Inuit and so they had affection for them but had great difficulty in understanding each other. The Pond Inlet people thought that the Inukjuak Inuit people were speaking in English because their dialects were different. The Inukjuak people never knew where the Pond Inlet people were going or what they were planning to do."[187]

SAMWILLIE ELIJASIALAK

Samwillie Elijasialak was born in the Inukjuak area in 1936 and relocated to Grise Fiord in 1953. He returned to Inukjuak in 1979. This is the translated account of his testimony:

> "He said that it is true of everyone that they had a special affection for their original homeland. They were completely satisfied with how life was treating them in their original homeland. It is not true that they were starving and living in poverty. He did not know of any extreme hunger when he was growing up but he did experience extreme hunger when he moved to the High Arctic. That was because in those locations there were no trade goods, there was no food or groceries available in any measure in the new locations.
>
> "The place that they moved to was absolutely desolate. The place where they put up camp was some distance from Craig Harbour. The police told them their camp was distant from Craig Harbour so that they would not be a burden on the police.
>
> "All of them were living with the pain resulting from this relocation and they never stopped pursuing solutions. The pain they felt in their hearts was the result of deception and being told lies or being promised things that nobody ever had any intention of fulfilling.
>
> "His mother and father told him what they were promised. They were promised plentiful caribou in the new land and that they would have freedom to return to their original homeland in two years if they so desired. What they found was very different. They were told right off that: 'you can only catch one caribou per year for your family. That's the regulation.' And that 'You are not allowed to kill any Musk-ox.' He wonders why the police

even bothered mentioning caribou and musk-ox and the plenty-fullness of these animals when they were trying to recruit people....

"The freedom to return after two years also turned out to be a very big lie. The first groups who returned did so at their own expense, having to pay their own way.

"When our parents attempted to make a case for returning, they were told outright that there's no possible way for them to ever go back and in fact some government officials said 'If you want to return, you are going to have to find other people to take your place before we allow you to go back.'

"'My father lived for only eight months after the relocation to the High Arctic.' It had sunk into his father that it would probably never be possible again for him to return to his original homeland and that he had been told about plentiful wildlife was absolutely not true. He was severely depressed and died of a broken heart.

"Many of the older generation and adults suffered depression caused by broken promises and finding out what they were told was not true. Their lives were irreparably damaged by this.

"They did not ask to be moved. It was imposed on them. In those days, white people were feared and their word was taken as authority. It was believed not to be wise to counter the white people's wishes in those days.

"It hurts him to recall the people who were left behind and who would never be seen again. He remembers parting where those who were left behind were told not to worry because the people who were going would be back, but they never were going to see each other again."[188]

Relocation – For the Benefit of the Inuit or Canada?

The relocation of the Quebec Inuit to the High Artic has been highly controversial. The Inuit consider that the relocation was unnecessary, as they had no quarrel with their life at Inukjuak. They believed that they were not told of all of the factors involved in the move and therefore did not consent to it. The Inuit believed the government made promises they had no intention of keeping and that the primary reason for the relocation was to assert Canadian sovereignty in the High Arctic. The government said that the relocation was done for the good of the people affected and that sovereignty was not a factor. The government acknowledged that there was unforeseeable hardship endured by those affected, but it did not accept fiduciary responsibility for the relocation.

An unanswered question thus remains. Was the protection of Canada's territorial sovereignty the main reason for the relocation of the Inuit from Inukjuak to the High Arctic or was it, as stated, for the benefit of the Inuit? The Canadian government expressed its concern over ownership of the High Arctic for a number of years preceding the 1953 and 1955relocations. It was aware that hunters from Greenland had been hunting on Ellesmere Island for a number of years without asking Canada's permission to do so. In addition, there was growing concern that the United States might start claiming territorial possession in Canada's north because of its military and transportation bases that were established there during the Second World War.

These concerns over sovereignty had been expressed a number of times prior to the time of the relocations in the early 1950s. Diamond Jenness, in lectures at the RCAF Staff College in 1944 and 1945, stated: "There can be no doubt that Canada would immensely strengthen her claim to sovereignty over the uninhabited islands in her Arctic sector if she established either Eskimo settlements or (and) scientific research stations on those islands that are most accessible by sea or air." In a report to the Department of Mines and Resources dated June 22, 1948, Jenness further stated: "The Department may decide to educate and train the Inuit population, among other things to colonize those areas, now uninhabited, in which it may be advisable to establish permanent settlements in order to assert and vindicate Canadian sovereignty."[189]

The Royal Commission on Aboriginal Peoples examined the question of sovereignty in the decision to relocate the Inukjuak Inuit. Their conclusions were ambiguous: "The weight of evidence points to sovereignty as a material consideration in the relocation decision. There is also some evidence to indicate that sovereignty was a consideration in the decision to continue the Grise Fiord settlement. It is also clear that the relocation did contribute to the maintenance of Canadian sovereignty in the Arctic." The Commission's report continued: "Even if sovereignty is assumed not to be a factor, this relocation was an inappropriate solution to the government's economic and social concerns. Sovereignty was, however, a material consideration, and the influence of sovereignty on the relocation serves only to reinforce the Commission's conclusion about the inappropriateness of the relocation. However, the precise extent to which sovereignty influenced the relocation is difficult to determine."[190]

THE ONGOING CONTROVERSY

Controversy remains about the relocation of the Quebec Inuit to the High Arctic and its aftermath. Some government officials and others involved in the relocation process have been critical of the investigations conducted, and they believe that they have been treated unfairly. At the same time, collateral effects on those involved in the relocation are now becoming visible.

In their examination of the High Arctic Relocation that occurred in 1953 and 1955, the Royal Commission on Aboriginal Peoples heard testimonies from the affected relocatees as well as government officials, the RCMP, and others who were involved in planning and in implementation. In general, and in opposition to the testimony provided by the relocatees, the government officials and others testified that the relocation had been successful, had been conducted in the best interests of the Inuit, and that the negative aspects related by the relocatees were exaggerated, possibly in an effort to extract compensation from the government. They also believed that the Inuit participated in the relocation voluntarily, that no offer to return to their original homes was ever made, and that the question of sovereignty was not a factor in the decision to relocate. In addition, the RCMP, who were posted to look after the Inuit in the High Arctic, said that they believed the relocatees were satisfied with their treatment as they were always smiling and always shaking their hands.[191]

In his testimony, Gordon Robertson, who was a member of the Privy Council Office from 1949 to 1953 and Deputy Minister of the Department of Resources and Development and also Commissioner of the Northwest Territories effective November 15, 1953, testified that the decision on the relocation was made in Ottawa without participation by the Inuit. He said: "I don't know that the Inuit would have suggested anything different. I don't suppose that they had the capacity at that time to judge what could be different. I don't know, but in any event, it didn't happen."[192] In her book *The Long Exile,* Melanie McGrath quotes Robertson as saying that the Royal Commission hearings were a "travesty of justice which had wantonly destroyed the reputation of the civil servants involved."[193]

Gerald Kenney, in his book *Arctic Smoke & Mirrors,* takes the position that the Royal Commission on the relocation was flawed and biased in favour of the Inuit. Kenney held that his research showed that the government's actions were for "the wellbeing of the Inuit living on the stark and unproductive 'hungry coast' on the eastern side of Hudson's Bay. Inukjuak was one of these communities. I found much written evidence to show that that part of the north was indeed an area of inadequate resources and destitution." With respect to the High Arctic communities, Kenney stated: "While the Inuit have said that they were hungry and underwent terrible sufferings in their new High Arctic homes after relocations, I found no evidence of this. What I did find was plenty of documentation showing that the Inuit thought they were far better off in their new homes than they ever had in Inukjuak, that they had more food and fur resources."[194]

Alan Marcus in his book *Out in the Cold: The Legacy of Canada's Inuit Relocation Experiment in the High Arctic* states that the relocation operation was developed as a colonization plan, making the new colonies at Grise Fiord and Resolute Bay the northernmost Inuit settlements in Canada.[195] With respect to the question of whether the Inuit volunteered or were ordered to relocate, Marcus said: "The Inuit did not request the relocation; working under the aegis of a 'rehabilitation' scheme, officials found 'volunteers' to fill their quotas. The Inuit did not volunteer to be separated on board the *C.D. Howe*, an action which was executed without advance consultation. The Inuit did not volunteer to be taken by the RCMP to a site sixty-five km away from the detachment and store at Craig Harbour and placed on a narrow beach with few provisions. The Inuit did not volunteer to be permanently separated from extended families and friends at Port Harrison (Inukjuak). The Inuit did not volunteer to be placed in small communities of closely related people and to have to undergo the subsequent difficulties of searching for spouses. Though involved in the planning, the Department of Northern Affairs and National Resources (Department) abdicated operational responsibility to the RCMP, allowing the relocatees to be placed in isolated colonies under the sole tutelage of police officers, without the moderating influence of permanently stationed personnel from the Department or other agencies. Nor did the Inuit volunteer to be removed from a ready source of health care, a school and other services at Port Harrison."[196]

In a 1952 First Conference on Eskimo Affairs held in Ottawa, no Inuit were invited to contribute to discussions on what decisions the government should take about their future. Col. Cunningham was reported to have explained the department's view to a member of the public: "The only reason why Eskimos were not invited to the meetings, was apart from the difficulties of transportation and language, that it was felt that few, if any, of them have yet reached the stage they could take responsible part in such discussions."[197]

Martha Flaherty, daughter of Josephie Flaherty and granddaughter of Robert Flaherty, who filmed and produced the documentary *Nanook of the North,* lived for two years with her parents at Resolute Bay on Ellesmere Island until her father died. Moving south, she was able to attend school, and in later life, made periodic trips to Resolute Bay. According to Flaherty, alcoholism was widespread amongst the Inuit with liquor provided by the military personnel stationed at the Canadian Air Force base located there. There was interaction between the men stationed at the base and Inuit women resulting, according to Flaherty, in a number of children being born to single Inuit women who had to take care of them after the Air Force personnel left the base.[198]

From what may have appeared to the government planners of the relocation scheme as an interesting experiment in human adaptability came results that adversely affected generations of Inuit individuals and their families. The High Artic relocation was a government-driven, internal colonization scheme with dire consequences.

ACKNOWLEDGEMENT OF WRONGDOING AND APOLOGIES

The Royal Commission on Aboriginal Peoples made a number of recommendations at the conclusion of its 1994 report. They were that the government acknowledge the wrongs done to the Inuit, apologize to the relocates, acknowledge the special contribution of the relocatees to the maintenance of Canadian sovereignty in the High Arctic, and compensate the relocatees for their suffering and abuse.[199]

The government refused to apologize but established a Reconciliation Agreement in March 1996. The agreement created a $10 million trust fund for relocated families. The government admitted that the Inuit had suffered hardship and loss in the initial years of the relocations but did not admit guilt. The agreement required the recipients of any compensation to agree that the government undertook the relocation for the best interests of the Inuit.[200]

Some fifteen years later, on August 18, 2010, the government made an official apology. Minister of Indian Affairs and Northern Development John Duncan stated: "The government of Canada deeply regrets the mistakes and broken promises of the dark chapter in our history and apologizes for the High Arctic relocation having taken place. We would like to pay tribute to the relocatees for their perseverance and courage… The relocation of Inuit families to the High Arctic is a tragic chapter in Canada's history that we should not forget, but that we must acknowledge, learn from and teach our children. Acknowledging our shared history allows us to move forward in partnership and in a spirit of reconciliation."[201]

The Nunavut Ahiarmiut Relocations

Starting in 1949 and continuing during the 1950s, the Canadian government forced Ahiarmiut peoples living in their ancestral homes in southwestern Nunavut to relocate to several locations where they were left to fend for themselves, without any shelter and tools needed for survival. The relocations occurred over several years and included a number of communities. People were moved from near Ennadai Lake to Nueltin Lake, and then to Henik Lake, Arviat and then Whale Cove and Rankin Inlet.

The Ahiarmiut People

The Ahiarmiut are an inland Inuit people that, prior to relocation, lived in the Ennadai Lake region that is within the Kivaliq Region of present-day Nunavut. The word Ahiarmiut can be translated as the "Out-of-the-Way Dwellers." They relied on the caribou for their basic subsistence, which was variable, depending on the route the caribou took for their spring and fall migrations.

One of their first contacts with Europeans was in 1893 when Joseph Tyrrell, working on behalf of the Geological Survey of Canada, reported there were approximately 2,000 "Caribou Eskimos" living in that area. In the 1930s, Hudson Bay Company post managers reported that the Ahiarmiut numbered around eighty.[202] In their book *Tammamiit, Inuit Relocation in the Eastern Artic,* F.J. Tester and Peter Kulchyski estimated that in the 1950s there were some fifty-five Ahiarmiut men, women, and children living in the Ennadai Lake region.[203]

The Relocations

Following World War II, the Canadian Army built a military radio station at Ennadai Lake. Government officials speculated that the Ahiarmiut who lived in the vicinity would start relying on the station as a source of food during food shortages as the result of inadequate caribou availability. The decision was made to relocate the Ahiarmiut population to another location, further away from the station. Without consultation with the Ahiarmiut and without any joint planning with them, government representatives arrived at the site. David Serkoak, now an Elder, but who was a child of one of the families involved, related the experiences encountered, as told to him by Elders: "Three men came from the radio station – a heavy equipment operator, an extra man and a police man. The Ahairmiut were ordered out of their tents… and the order was given to bulldoze their stuff back and forth and bury it. And another signal was given to get on a plane.

And, away we went to Nueltin Lake. The group was not provided with tents on arrival and slept outside. There were a few elderly people who did not make it."[204]

In the winter of the same year, the Ahiarmiut decided to return to Ennadai Lake on their own, by walking back to their original community. It took them three months to do so. However, they were again forced to relocate by government officials, this time to Henik Lake, again without consultation or approval. Due to the absence of caribou, food at Henik Lake was scarce and resulted in starvation and conflict within the group. The surviving Ahiarmiut at Henik Lake were airlifted to Arviat in early 1959. From there, they were later relocated several additional times, to Whale Cove, then to Itivia and then back to Whale Cove.

Throughout each of these moves, hardship was inflicted on the Ahiarmiut, which resulted in the premature loss of life, destruction of family ties, and growing tension and conflict within their communities. There were no positive outcomes in the relocation schemes carried out by Canadian government officials. Yet, senior government officials were well aware of the tragedies that were occurring. Midway through the relocation period, Graham Rowley, secretary of the Advisory Committee on Northern Development, wrote two memoranda to his deputy minister.

In the first memo, Rowley wrote: "Moves have rarely been successful unless they are done with the full consent of the people concerned. To us, one part of the barrens may appear very much like another, but this is not the case with the Eskimos. The region in which they have lived for many years has associations which mean a great deal to them, and detailed knowledge of any area is essential for hunters who wish to exploit its potential fully. In view of the fact that these Eskimos liked the Ennadai region and did not want to leave it, it appeared unlikely that the move was accepted by them."[205]

In his second memo, Rowley said: "It seems clear that only two years ago the Eskimo were happy and content at Ennadai. The deterioration which appears to have settled in is certainly owing in part to their moving to unfamiliar surroundings. Another reason is probably lack of discipline which resulted from weakening the normal tribal procedures. Among the Eskimo in general, and specifically this tribe, decisions on moving a camp are reached after considerable discussion within the tribe… The decision to move to Henik Lake, initiated from the outside, cannot have failed to weaken the authority of those who usually decide these things, and may have contributed to the general despondency reported in the area."[206]

Government Apology and Financial Settlement

On January 22, 2019, the Government of Canada made a formal apology to the Ahiarmiut for the multiple relocations that they had endured. In the apology, the government admitted it operated with a "colonial mindset." The apology was delivered by the Honourable Carolyn Bennett, Minister of Crown-Indigenous Relations. The following are some of her remarks:

"Nearly seventy years ago, the Government of Canada relocated the Ahiarmuit for the first time, moving your people from their homeland at Ennadai Lake to Nuelten Lake. This relocation was undertaken without explanation, without consultation, and without consent. The Ahiarmiut were moved in a matter of hours. Families were directed onto an airplane and flown to an island in Nueltin Lake. They were forced to leave behind their territory, their shelters, and most of their belongings, including tools critical to survival such as axes, knives and outdoor clothing. Once at Nueltin Lake, Canada did not provide the Ahiarmiut with adequate food, shelter, tools or other supplies. They had no shelters and no caribou skins to build new ones. There was insufficient food on the island to sustain the people. What assistance they received came, not from government officials, but from Dene hunters in the area, who shared some food and supplies."[207]

With respect to later relocations, the minister said: "Starving families at North Henik and Oftedal Lakes were forced to eat what little they could find: Caribou hides stripped of fur, a single ptarmigan shared among ten children, one fish cut into tiny pieces to last a family several days. Malnourished mothers were unable to nurse their own infants."[208]

The minister's concluding remarks included the following: "The relocations of the Ahiarmiut between 1950 and 1960 were misguided, mishandled and tragic. These relocations profoundly and permanently impacted Ahiarmiut community members and the Ahiarmiut way of life… We now understand that the Government of Canada moved the Ahairmiut from your homeland based on a colonial mindset that ignored your deep ties to the lands and the wisdom gleaned from your ancestors."[209]

The settlement amount, as reported by the CBC, was $5 million for survivors of the relocations and their children. Each survivor was promised $100,000 and each child of the survivors was to receive $3,000.[210]

Sayisi Dene Relocation in Manitoba

Before being relocated, the Sayisi Dene (People of the East) lived a mainly nomadic caribou-hunting existence in an area of northern Manitoba and southern Northwest Territories. With the arrival of the fur traders, they augmented their equipment and supplies by trading with the Hudson's Bay Company at what is now Churchill, Manitoba. The Sayisi Dene spent their winters scattered across the region, living in tents and small cabins, trapping, fishing, and hunting caribou that followed traditional migration routes. Their main settlement was at Little Duck Lake. In the early 1950s, a provincial government biologist who was visiting the area reported what he thought was over-killing of the caribou. Rumours were started that there was, or would be, a food shortage. Later studies, however, concluded this was not the case and that there was ample food in the area for use by the Sayisi Dene. Acting on colonial instinct, both the provincial and federal governments decided, without consultation with the Sayisi Dene, that they would be relocated to a location near Churchill.

The relocation, by government plane, took place on August 17, 1956. The Sayisi Dene were required to settle on a barren tundra location some fifteen kilometres outside of Churchill. And, as was the case with the Ahiarmiut Nunavut relocation, equipment required for daily living, such as boats, traps, sleds, and their dogs, was left behind. According to a 1973 report by Indian and Northern Affairs Canada, the relocation was done without "adequate understanding, assent or preparation."[211] At first, the community members lived in shacks and tents. They were later moved to government-built homes at a location called Camp 10. After living at Camp 10 for about ten years, the community was again moved, to a new site 6.5 kilometres south of Churchill, called Dene Village. The newly built houses at this site proved to be unsatisfactory for the winter conditions at

Churchill, with the result that they became inhabitable some five years later. Some community members began leaving the village on their own and moved back to their native lands. By 1977, most of the Dene Village community had relocated to Taboule Lake in north-central Manitoba, about 250 kilometres west of Churchill. By this time, however, 117 of the more than 250 members who were involved in the original move had died.[212]

In 2010, the province of Manitoba formally apologized for its role in the original relocation and offered 13,000 acres of Crown land as compensation for the negative effects of the relocations. On August 16, 2016, Indigenous and Northern Affairs Minister Carolyn Bennett apologized for the federal government's role in the relocations at a ceremony held at Taboule Lake, and she announced the government would provide the First Nation some $33 million in compensation that included individual survivor payments of $15,000 to $20,000 per person.[213]

Section 2

Colonialism by Direct Attack and Subjugation

Chapter 6

Colonialism and Its Deadly Consequences - the Tsilhqot'in War and the North-West Rebellion

COLONIZING COUNTRIES HAVE USUALLY DEALT HARSHLY WITH THE INDIGenous peoples of their conquered lands. Spain treated its South American subjects with brute force as did the French with the peoples of Haiti. The British treated their Indian subjects with force and disdain. The Canadian government's record in dealing with internal colonization, before and after Confederation, has also been harsh. This chapter presents examples of the government's actions against Canada's Indigenous Peoples in British Columbia and in Saskatchewan. The military and police actions against the First Nations and Metis peoples occurred in a relatively short period of time, but the outcomes were drastic. Fourteen First Nations chiefs and one Metis leader were executed by hanging. And there is the lingering question as to whether those executed were criminals or defenders of their territories and just seeking what had been promised to them under treaties and in agreements.

Tsilhqot'in (Chilcotin) War

The Tsilhqot'in War occurred in 1864 on the Chilcotin Plateau, which is near present-day Williams Lake, located in the interior of British Columbia. The estimated population of BC at that time was some 7,000 white persons and an estimated 60,000 First Nations people.[214] Access to the Chilcotin Plateau area from New Westminster was by the Fraser River valley, a lengthy and costly route. A businessman by the name of Alfred Waddington was behind a project to build a new road to access the mineral deposits in the area. Waddington's proposed route utilized the Bute Inlet along BC's west coast with a road from the end of the Inlet to the Chilcotin Plateau area. The new road would have shortened the existing access route to the potential mines by a substantial amount. Waddington had obtained the necessary approvals from the jurisdictional colonial government but had not negotiated approval from the First Nations over whose land the road would cross.

The Tsilhqot'in and other First Nations in the area were, at that time, short of food and had just gone through a devastating episode of smallpox. Overall, it was estimated that a third of the total native population in BC had died from the disease and, in the case of the Tsilhqot'in, over one-half of the population died.[215] The Tsilhqot'in and other First Nation peoples in the area were concerned that the new road through their territory would expose them to another episode of smallpox and other European diseases. In addition, they felt betrayed by the white community because it had not offered to share in the financial rewards that the exploitation of the natural resources on their lands would produce. They were also concerned that the increased activity would drive away wild game upon which they relied for food.[216]

On April 29, 1864, a ferryman working some fifty kilometres downstream from the road construction site was killed by Tsilhqot'in members when he refused to share some of the food he had. The next day at dawn the Tsilhqot'in attacked the construction camp, which was located on Tsilhqot'in land, killing twelve workers. Further attacks occurred the next day so that, in total, twenty-one men were killed. The Tsilhqot'in maintained that the killings occurred as part of the war they were engaged in with the white society and that had been brought about by infringement on their land without permission. [217]

The killings created a major challenge for colonial governor Frederick Seymour. Several unsuccessful attempts were made by militia and others over the ensuing months to reach the area and arrest the men responsible for the killings. In July, Seymour made contact with Tsilhqot'in Chief Alexis through Gold Commissioner William Cox, , proposing that the two sides should meet to discuss the event. Alexis agreed to meet with the understanding that the Tsilhqot'in chiefs would be meeting with Seymour, the meeting would be safe, and they would be granted immunity. Cox had, through a mediator, sent a gift of tobacco to the Tsilhqot'in chiefs, a traditional sign of peace that meant that no harm would come to them. The next day, eight native representatives arrived as planned, but five were immediately arrested and charged with murder.[218]

The five Tsilhqot'in were tried at Quesnellmouth that September with Judge Begbie presiding. During the abbreviated trial, the defendants said that they were waging war and not committing murder. The five were found guilty of murder and sentenced to be hanged.[219]

Governor Seymour, in a dispatch to London, acknowledged validity to the position that there was a war between the whites and the Tsilhqot'in when he said: "There was no use any longer shutting my eyes to the fact, this was a war merciless on one side, and in which we were engaged with the greater part of the Chilcotin nation."[220] Judge Begbie expressed the view that the whites had shown poor judgment: "The Indians have, I believe, been injudiciously treated. If a sound discretion had been exercised towards them, I believe this outrage would not have been perpetrated."[221] Judge Begbie concluded that "the most important cause of the unrest was concern over title to the land rather than plunder or revenge."[222]

On October 26, 1884, the five Tsilhqot'in leaders—Klatassine, Tellot, Tahpitt, Piel, and Chessus were executed by hanging at Quenellemouth. A year later, on July 15, 1865, a sixth Tsilhqot'in chief, Ahan, was executed by hanging at New Westminster.[223]

In 1993, the British Columbia government conducted an inquiry into the relationship between the Aboriginal community and the justice system. As a result of the recommendations in the inquiry report, the province's attorney general apologized for the hanging of the Tsilhqot'in chiefs. In 2014, the British Columbia government exonerated the Tsilhqot'in leaders. Premier Christy Clark stated: "We confirm without reservation that these Chilcotin chiefs are fully exonerated for any crimes or wrongdoing."[224] On March 26, 2018, Prime Minister Justin Trudeau offered an official exoneration for the Tsilhqot'in men hanged in 1864 and 1865. Trudeau said: "We recognize that these chiefs were leaders of a nation, that they acted in accordance with their laws and traditions and that they are well regarded as heroes of their people."[225]

The aftermath of the Tsilhqot'in war was that the road was never built. To this day, much of the traditional Tsilhqot'in land has been left untouched through settlement or other intrusion. And, in a case heard by the Supreme Court of Canada in 2014, the Tsilhqot'in First Nation was awarded title to some 1,700 square kilometres of land near Williams Lake.[226]

North-West Rebellion/Resistance

The North-West Rebellion is sometimes referred to as the North-West Resistance. From the government's side, it was a rebellion against the government and its agencies. From the Metis and First Nations' point of view, it was an act of resistance against the intrusion of their territory and way of life and a danger to their survival. For fairness, we will use both terms.

There were two elements of the Rebellion/Resistance, with some overlap between them. The primary battles between the Metis and mainly government troops took place near and at Batoche in what is now Saskatchewan. Other distinctive battles between First Nations and authorities took place both in Saskatchewan and Alberta. In the battle at Batoche, some First Nations peoples participated with the Metis while some Metis participated with First Nations in their battles.

The Metis Conflicts

Because of the unsatisfactory result of the Red River Rebellion that took place in Manitoba in 1869-1870, many of the Metis from that region relocated to the communities of Batoche, Fish Creek, St. Louis, St. Laurent, and Duck Lake, all on or near the South Saskatchewan River in what is now Saskatchewan. While they knew the buffalo herds were diminishing, they felt that they had a better chance of survival in their new location and also thought that they could be granted lands on which to farm. However, with the construction of railways and the influx of European farm settlers, the government began surveying the land and granting title to the new immigrants and others. As had been the case at the Red River settlement in Manitoba, the Metis divided the lands they occupied on the seigneurial basis with strips of land reaching back from the river, similar to the traditional system they had been accustomed to in Quebec. However, the government surveyed the lands on the "section" basis. As a result, in 1883, after the surveys were completed, thirty-six families of the parish of St. Louis found that their land and village, which included a church and a school, had been sold by the Government of Canada to the Prince Albert Colonization Company. Not having title to the land they occupied, the Metis feared losing them all.[227]

Based on their experience in Manitoba, in 1884, the Metis asked Louis Riel to return from the United States, where he had fled after the unsuccessful Red River Rebellion, and petition the government to grant the Metis land, as was the case with the reserve system implemented with the First Nations. Riel's efforts went unheeded. As a result, Gabriel Dumont and others set up the Provisional Government of Saskatchewan, using similar tactics to those used in Manitoba that were the forerunner of the formation of the Province of Manitoba. At the same time, though unrelated with the Metis concerns, a number of Cree nations began agitating, with violence in some cases, because of food shortages and the unfulfilled federal government promises that had been included in the signed treaties. Planning for the possibility of conflict, the federal government began mobilizing the Canadian militia in Winnipeg under the command of Major-General Frederick Middleton.[228]

The first military action occurred on March 26, 1885, at Duck Lake, west of Batoche. An estimated 150 to 200 Metis and some First Nations under the command of Gabriel Dumont defeated a combined force of some ninety personnel, comprised of North-West Mounted Police and civilian volunteers from Prince Albert. The battle was short-lived, but three police officers and nine volunteers were killed. The Metis lost five men. Following the battle at Duck Lake, the government hastened its military deployment of troops and increased their number by including personnel from Toronto and Montreal. By May, Middleton had a force of 3,000 troops, along with 2,000 volunteers and 500 North-West Mounted Police.[229]

The next battle occurred at Fish Creek (Tourond's Coulee) on April 24. Middleton's forces approached Batoche from the south, travelling along both the eastern and western shores of the South Saskatchewan River. At the small community of Fish Creek, on the east shore of the river, about twenty kilometres south of Batoche, Middleton's force of some 900 soldiers encountered a Metis force estimated at 200 men. The Metis attacked Middleton's forces to stop their march north. They were successful and forced the advancing army to retreat. Six soldiers were killed and forty-nine wounded in the skirmish. The Metis lost four men.[230]

On May 9, 1885, Middleton, with a reinforced army and a steamship acting as a gun boat on the South Saskatchewan River, attacked Batoche, the Metis's main centre. The Metis had established a network of defensive trenches and pits that initially stopped Middleton's army's advance. However, after three days of combat, the Metis ran out of ammunition and were forced to surrender. An estimated fifty-one Metis were killed in battle, with many dispersing. Middleton reported that eight of his soldiers were killed in the battle. On May 15, Louis Riel, himself, surrendered, while Dumont and other participants fled south across the United States border into Montana Territory.

Was the Canadian government an eager participant in instigating the 1885 Metis conflicts, or was it only reacting to circumstances created by others? This question has been examined by Don McLean in his book *1885 Metis Rebellion or Government Conspiracy?*[231]

As noted, many of the Metis who were involved in the 1885 conflict with federal government militia and police in the Batoche area of Saskatchewan came from the Red River area of Manitoba. Based on their experiences there, they knew that they had to be organized and prepared to deal with the federal government if they were to obtain recognition as a distinct community that included land rights. As early as 1873, the Metis community at St. Laurent developed a set of rules, known as the "Laws of St. Laurent," that governed living rights and responsibilities. In particular, the rules set out procedures governing food security and buffalo hunting. In addition, the Metis prepared and submitted petitions to the federal government, requesting dialogue with respect to land and other rights. The federal government, for the most part, ignored these communications. In November 1884, the Metis prepared a "Bill of Rights" and forwarded it to the federal government for discussion, but they did not receive any response. As time passed, the Metis became more concerned as they observed that much of the land was being surveyed and sold. In order to bring the matter to the attention of the Federal government, they asked for the assistance of Louis Riel.

At the same time, the Macdonald government was proceeding with its National Plan that included the construction of the Canadian Pacific Railway (CPR) to service the prairies and beyond the Rocky Mountains. However, the CPR was running into financial problems and requested additional financial support from the federal government to complete its work. The government was experiencing political resistance to any additional funding to the railway company. Coupled with its financial problems, the CPR decided to cross the prairies along a southern route instead of the anticipated northern route through the Prince Albert region of Saskatchewan. This decision greatly affected land speculators, who had purchased land adjacent to the proposed railway route, which included the Batoche area.

In his book, McLean postulates that Conservative Party officials and others in the Prince Albert area falsely proclaimed that the Metis were preparing for war in order to mobilize federal government militia from the east to fight the Metis. Because the fastest way to transport the militia was by railway, a need was created to have it supported financially and completed. While McLean offers no concrete evidence that the federal government was a participant in the scheme, he does suggest reasons why it would have been supportive of the events that took place.

The First Nations Encounters

In 1885, the First Nations were suffering from hunger largely due to the disappearance of the buffalo, their traditional main source of food. At the same time, the federal government was not fulfilling its promise of providing adequate support, as it had agreed to under the treaties. Leaders of the First Nations and others decided that they had to take some form of action. This resulted in several incidents that developed into conflict between the First Nations and the white population and law-enforcement agencies.

The first such incident occurred on March 30, 1885, when Chief Poundmaker approached the community of Battleford. The purpose of the visit was to request the Indian agent there, Mr. Rae, for food and supplies. Rae declined to meet with Poundmaker. The community's inhabitants, fearing a rumoured attack, fled to the nearby North-West Mounted Police post at Fort Battleford, abandoning their stores and homes. After waiting two days without success to meet with Rae and suffering from hunger, the Cree took food and supplies from the vacated properties and returned to their own communities.[232]

Three days later, on April 2, 1885, the Cree, led by war chief Wandering Spirit, attacked the small community of Frog Lake, which was located just west of the present-day Alberta–Saskatchewan border and north of present-day Lloydminster. The initial encounter escalated quickly when Chief Big Bear, frustrated by negotiations with government officials with respect to the reserve land allocated to his band and by the government withholding food, became angry. Bolstered by the favourable events at Duck Lake, Big Bear decided to apprehend some of the white settlers and others living in the area and hold them hostage in the local church. When discussions and negotiations with Thomas Quinn, the town's Indian Agent, broke down, Wandering Spirit shot and killed Quinn. Chief Big Bear tried to stop the violence, but the warriors took their own initiative and killed eight people, including two priests who were being held captive. A further three white settlers were kept in captivity.[233]

On April 15, 1885, 200 Cree warriors approached Fort Pitt, located east of present-day Lloydminster. They intercepted a police scouting party and opened fire, killing one officer and wounding another. Being outnumbered, the Fort's commanding officer Francis Dickens surrendered to the attackers and agreed to negotiate. Chief Big Bear decided to release the captured officers, but the Cree destroyed the fort. Dickens and his men reached safety at Battleford six days later.[234]

On May 2, 1885, troops from Fort Battleford raided the Cree community at Cut Knife, located forty kilometres west of Battleford. The raid has never been explained, but it is speculated to be in retribution against the Cree for camping near Battleford earlier in the year and displacing the people there. As was the Cree's custom, war chief Fine Day replaced political chief Poundmaker as leader until the fighting was over. The government troops had expected to fight the Cree on an open field where they had observed that tents were located. However, the Cree had moved into two wooded ravines where they had a field advantage over the militia. The result was that Fine Day successfully held off Lieutenant-Colonel William Otter and his men, despite Otter having the use of a Gatling gun and a larger number of soldiers. Though the Cree had an opportunity to kill many of the government forces, Poundmaker intervened and allowed them to retreat and return to Fort Battleford. Otter reported losing eight men with fourteen wounded, while five native warriors were killed and three wounded.[235]

On May 28, 1885, Major-General Thomas Strange led a force of some 1,000 men—cowboys, white settlers, and two units of North-West Mounted Police—originating from what is now Alberta, to attack a Cree settlement at Frenchman's Butte in present-day Saskatchewan. The Cree were led by war chief Wandering Spirit, who, with about 200 men, prepared for the attack by digging trenches and pits on high ground, forcing Strange's men to cross muskeg-bottomed valleys. Gunfire was exchanged for about three hours, after which Strange pulled his troops back and retreated. A number of militia and Cree warriors were wounded, with one Cree warrior killed in the battle.[236]

The battle at Loon Lake was the last battle recorded between the First Nations and government forces. Major Sam Steele led a force of North-West Mounted Police and Alberta Mounted Rifles against a band of Cree led by Big Bear at Loon Lake, near Frenchman's Butte. After an initial exchange of fire, the Cree ran out of ammunition and dispersed, suffering four dead and many wounded.[237]

Trials, Incarceration, and Executions

Retribution by the Canadian government against the First Nations and Metis leaders was swift and severe. During the summer of 1885, the government charged eighty-one First Nation and Metis, who had been captured or had surrendered, with arson, theft, murder, and treason felonies. The initial trials took place in Regina with Magistrate Hugh Richardson presiding. The trials then moved to Battleford, where eleven men were charged with murder.[238]

FIRST NATION INCARCERATIONS AND EXECUTIONS

Following the Regina trials, forty-four First Nation convicted prisoners were imprisoned at the Manitoba Penitentiary (now Stoney Mountain). Included were Cree Chiefs Big Bear, Poundmaker, and One Arrow. Big Bear and Poundmaker were released prior to the end of their three-year prison sentences.

The trials held at Battleford for the eleven men charged with murder took on a higher profile. The presiding magistrate, Charles Rouleau, wanted to convey the message that the accused were to be judged on their deeds, not their race. He was quoted as telling the accused: "If a white man murders an Indian, he must hang and so must an Indian if he kills a white man." The magistrate thus set aside any arguments of mitigating circumstances. Three of the men were charged with the murder of a Cree woman, She-Win; they claimed she was becoming a "Wendigo." Two of the men, Charlebois and Dressy Man, were found guilty of murder and were sentenced to death. The third man, Bright Eyes, was found guilty of manslaughter and was sentenced to life imprisonment. Charlebois's and Dressy Man's death penalties were later reprieved.[239] The remaining eight of the accused were found guilty of murder and were sentenced to death by hanging. They were Wandering Spirit, Little Bear, Around the Sky, Bad Arrow, Miserable Man, Iron Body, Itka, and Man Without Blood.[240]

The simultaneous executions by hanging of the eight convicted men took place in Battleford on November 27, 1885, on scaffolding built for the occasion. According to researcher Ted McCoy: "The hanging was carefully planned as a public spectacle at Fort Battleford to demonstrate visibly the government's power over First Nation people. Prime Minister John A. Macdonald, also acting as Minister of Indian Affairs, informed (Indian Commissioner) Dewdney, "the executions.... ought to convince the Red Man that the White Man governs." Assistant Indian Commissioner Hayter Reed agreed with the prime minister and suggested to Dewdney that First Nations people must witness the hangings as confirmation of their "sound thrashing."[241] McCoy goes on to say: "Canada's legal response to the convicted First Nations participants suggests that, beneath an overarching colonial agenda, the law operated in complex and contradictory ways. The Rebellion court cases, capital punishment, and penitentiary sentences reveal a process of colonialization in which the majesty, justice and mercy of the law unfolded, although seldom in the manner legal authorities intended. Elements of punishment, including execution and incarceration, demonstrate the different ways law and punishment were used to subordinate First Nations people."[242]

METIS INCARCERATIONS AND AN EXECUTION

Following the initial trials in Regina, thirty-six Metis prisoners who were convicted of various charges were transferred to Manitoba Penitentiary to serve out their sentences. Louis Riel, who was charged with high treason, received special attention. Riel's trial began in July 1885 in Regina. Riel and his lawyers asked for a political trial, but they were refused. Because of Riel's deteriorating mental state, his lawyers argued he should be found not guilty because of insanity. Riel, however, spoke in his own defence, in an eloquent and spiritual manner.

At his trial, Riel was accused of "[t]aking up arms at Duck Lake, Fish Creek and Batoche, both as a British subject and a visitor violating his local allegiance."[243] During the trial, the Secretary of State falsely denied that the Metis had submitted proposals on land and other claims for discussion with the government before taking up arms. Also at the trial, Catholic clergy from the Batoche and Duck Lake areas sided with the prosecution, blaming the conflict solely on Riel and others such as Gabriel Dumont and Napoleon Nault.[244]

Riel's trial lasted five days. The jury, after one hour of deliberation, found him guilty, but made a strong recommendation for mercy. However, the presiding judge ignored the recommendation and pronounced the sentence of death. There were, over the next weeks, several appeals to higher courts; all rejected leniency. A direct appeal to Prime Minister John A. Maconald was also rejected. Indeed, Macdonald was quoted as saying, "[h]e shall die, though every dog in Quebec bark in his favour."[245] Riel was hanged to death on November 16, 1885, in Regina.

Even at the time of Riel's trial, there were some who questioned the attitude and action taken by the government. During debate in the House of Commons, Sir Wilfrid Laurier said: "Had I been born on the banks of the Saskatchewan, I would myself have shouldered a musket to fight against the neglect of governments and the shameless greed of speculators."[246] As time progressed, Riel's contribution to the building of Canada was better understood and recognized, particularly in Manitoba where he has sometimes been called the founder of the Province of Manitoba.[247] His name has become associated with many organizations, such as the Louis Riel Teachers Association, Louis Riel Legacy Centre, Louis Riel School Division, all in Manitoba. The Province of Manitoba celebrates a Louis Riel Day, and there is a street named after him in Winnipeg. In Saskatchewan, the highway between Saskatoon and Prince Albert is called the Louis Riel Trail, and the Student's Union Centre at the University of Saskatchewan is named Place Riel.

Rebellion or Resistance?

In both the Tsilhqot'in War and the North-West Rebellion/Resistance, blood was shed by Indigenous Peoples, police officers, volunteers, and military personnel. There was, however, no satisfactory outcome. To a large extent, the root cause of these events remains to this day.

In the second half of the 1800s, Canada was going through a developmental stage, particularly in the west of the country. There was pressure to populate the west as part of the Canadian government's National Policy. This policy had two main objectives: creation of a national country to avoid intrusion by the Americans, and creation of markets for products manufactured in Ontario and Quebec. To populate the west with farmers, ranchers, and others, the government needed title to the land that was occupied by the region's Indigenous Peoples. As a means of extinguishing the Aboriginal titles of the native population, the government created the reserve system which forced First Nation peoples to live on designated parcels of lands owned by the Crown. In exchange, the government promised certain rights and support in education, health care, food supply, and means of making a living by supplying fishing gear and agricultural equipment. The reserves were owned by the Crown. Individuals living on them had no ownership rights.

In the case of the Metis, the government took a different approach. In order to extinguish the rights of the Metis people, it developed the scrip system. Under this system, each individual was given a scrip, or right, to a sum of money or to a parcel of land. If the individual Metis decided to use the land option, it was the government that decided where that land would be located. While the scrip policy was in place sometime before the events of the North-West Rebellion in 1885, it was only partially implemented. The result was the Metis residents at Batoche and Duck Lake had no legal recourse of ownership to the land they were living on and, in many cases, earning a living through farming.

As was, and is, typical of an internal colonial approach in dealing with domestic issues, the government turned to enforcement as a means of intervention rather than to a political solution. With this approach, problems are usually not solved, but postponed. Given that the results of the 1885 uprisings did not address the needs of the First Nation and Metis populations, the government failed to meet its legal and humanitarian obligations. The events of 1885 may have been based more on resistance than rebellion. History is showing that the First Nations and Metis leaders acted on behalf of their people and not for personal gain, making them more resistance fighters than criminals.

Section 3

Colonialism by Disdain, Disrespect, and Denial of Rights

Chapter 7

Colonialism by Neglect - Famine, Disease, Water Quality, and Flooding, Child Care, and Social Services

IN THE LATTER PART OF THE 1850S, A LARGE NUMBER OF FIRST NATION peoples were subjected to famine and deadly communicable diseases, such as smallpox, measles, cholera, scarlet fever, and tuberculosis. In the 1900s, much of the Inuit population was stricken with tuberculosis. In the 2000s, some First Nations people living in their communities on reserve land are still dealing with contaminated drinking water, poisoned rivers and lakes, and they are without adequate childcare support. While governments may not have caused these problems, they have been slow or even non-responsive in alleviating the inflicted miseries. In a sense, affected segments of Canada's population have and continue to be subjected to colonialism by neglect.

Famine with the Demise of the Bison

With the arrival of Europeans in North America, the health and traditional food supply of the Indigenous Peoples was greatly altered. The Europeans brought with them new diseases and a disregard for the traditional food sources that had sustained the indigenous population for centuries. The destruction of the great herds of bison that were the mainstay of the First Nations and Metis food source, especially on the prairies, caused famine and resulted in malnutrition that greatly increased the likelihood of death accompanying sickness caused by communicable disease.

Researchers have postulated that the North American bison originated in Asia and came to North America in two waves. The first wave occurred between 195,000 to 135,000 years ago, when the animals travelled from Siberia and entered North America across Beringia. The second wave occurred about 14,000 and 11,000 years ago, when the animals followed the same route. Two species of bison lived in North America—the plains and the wood. It is estimated that the plains bison, which lived in the central plains of Canada and the United States, numbered 30 million and the wood bison, which lived in the northern parts of the western Canadian provinces and territories, numbered an estimated 170,000.[248]

The depopulation of both plains and wood bison in Canada is directly attributed to the European colonization of North America as a result of the following circumstances:

- The increased need for domestic food to feed the fur traders and others that had taken up residence.
- The need for their hides, which were being exported to Europe for clothing and furniture and for industrial uses, such as belts used on motors and machinery and belts worn by soldiers.
- The intrusion into Canada by America natives for bison meat because the American military had slaughtered the bison in the United States to gain greater control of the native population there.
- The diseases that were infecting the native bison, brought to Canada by animals originating outside the country.
- The displacement of bison grazing areas, which the government was setting aside to accommodate settler's cattle.[249, 250]

The demise of the bison had a devastating effect on Canada's First Nations, especially those living on the prairies. It caused them to suffer starvation, which strongly influenced treaty negotiations, as the First

Nations were desperate to receive whatever assistance they could from the government. At the same time, the government did little, if anything, to save the bison herds—even though they knew that the herds were decreasing at an alarming rate. For example, as noted earlier, in the spring of 1874, the deputy minister of the interior reported that: "The buffaloes have in the last few years been rapidly diminishing in numbers, and there seems every reason to expect… they will within the next decade of years be entirely exterminated. To the Indians, extermination of the buffalo means starvation and death."[251]

Did the Canadian government have an obligation to protect the First Nations peoples against the demise of the bison and the famine that followed? From a legal point of view, only in the negotiations during Treaty No. 6 was famine included in the terms of agreement: "That in the event hereafter of the Indians comprised within this treaty being overcome by any pestilence, or by general famine, the Queen, on being satisfied and certified thereof by Her Indian Agent or Agents, will grant to the Indians assistance of such character and to such extent as Her Chief Superintendent of Indians Affairs shall deem necessary and sufficient to relieve the Indians from the calamity that shall have befallen them."[252] From a moral point of view, did the terms of Treaty No. 6 apply by inference to all of the treaties and/or did First Nations people, as subjects of the Crown, deserve to be protected from starvation?

Diseases - Smallpox and Tuberculosis

As noted, the arrival of Europeans in North America brought with them diseases for which the Indigenous population had no immunity. The two most deadly and devastating were smallpox and tuberculosis.

Smallpox

Smallpox was brought to North America in 1520 by the Spaniards on a ship that landed in Mexico. The disease immediately spread north along the coastal regions of the United States and Canada and south into South America. By the time Spanish conqueror Francisco Pizarro fought the Inca in Peru in 1532, the disease had already spread, killing thousands of native inhabitants. Smallpox is a highly infectious viral disease that usually enters the body through the nose and throat, then enters the lungs and lymphatic system. Without immunization, it is very deadly.

The First Nation populations in British Columbia were decimated by smallpox on at least two separate occasions. The first occurred in the 1770 to 1780 period and affected people living along the west coast, both in the north and south of the province. The results were catastrophic. The close confines of the winter homes provided ideal conditions for the disease to spread. It was reported that people died at such a rate that it became impossible to bury the dead according to tradition. This led to mass graves, but eventually, they too became unmanageable, resulting in the dead being left where they died. Community members who fled to avoid the sickness took the virus with them, spreading the disease.[253]

The second major smallpox epidemic occurred in March 1862. A ship carrying passengers from San Francisco docked in Victoria for a one-night layover. Most of the ship's passengers were gold seekers on their way to join the Cariboo Gold Rush. However, at least one of the passengers was carrying the smallpox virus and infected a First Nation person who visited the dock area where the passengers had disembarked. About one month after this event, the First Nation communities established near Victoria began experiencing a smallpox outbreak. As the disease spread, Victoria residents began to panic. Instead of assisting the First Nation population in combating the disease, the authorities ordered them to leave the area. The order was expanded to include all First Nations occupying the south-eastern portion of Vancouver Island. On June 11, 1862, the police commissioner, with a force of police officers, forced some 300 men, women, and children camped near Victoria to relocate north. A gunboat towed some twenty-six canoes full of people north to Fort Rupert, a fifteen-day trip.[254] It has been estimated that over 15,000 First Nation people living along the coast of British Columbia died of smallpox during this epidemic.[255]

In addition to entering Canada along the west coast, smallpox also entered the country along the east coast and then spread inland. By 1635, it had entered the St. Lawrence River valley system; it reached Sault Sainte Marie by 1702. From there, it moved into Manitoba and reached present-day Saskatchewan in 1780 where it surfaced at a Hudson Bay Company store located at Cumberland House, the first community established in the province. The company's agent at Cumberland House, William Tomison, kept a detailed diary of how smallpox spread and its devastating effect on the First Nation population in the area. He observed that survival depended upon isolation, and he encouraged the First Nation groups to isolate themselves as much as possible.[256]

In addition to these western and eastern vectors, smallpox also travelled north into Canada from the south. The disease established itself throughout the United States plains and spread north, particularly following the Missouri River system where it eventually affected the Red River system in Canada. Fortunately for some of the First Nations in Canada, the Hudson's Bay Company provided vaccines to them as well as to their own employees. As a result, some First Nations were less affected than others. But in the case of the Assiniboine and Niitsitapi, whose territories originated at the US – Canada border, the loss was so extensive that both First Nations were almost completely wiped out. In 1848, Paul Kane reported that he saw "[b]ones of a whole camp of Indians, who were carried off by the fatal scourge of their race – smallpox."[257] The loss of life in other parts of the country was also very high. Hudson Bay Commissioner Simpson in 1841 reported that the Sikiska, who lived near the Battle River in Saskatchewan, moved to the Blackfoot Crossing on the Bow River after losing half of their population to smallpox. In addition, Simpson estimated that the Sarcee's population declined from 1,800 to 250 because of the disease.[258]

Other than occasional help from Hudson Bay Company personnel, the First Nations were left, during most of the 1880s, to fight the disease on their own and without any government assistance. Other than the limited vaccinations they received, their main defence was to isolate themselves and refrain from contacting Europeans and fellow First Nations who had become infected.

Tuberculosis

Tuberculosis was widespread in pockets throughout Canada for many years, but it reached epidemic proportions amongst the First Nation and Inuit populations. This disease spreads and flourishes where there is poorly ventilated, crowded housing, and an inadequate, unbalanced diet. Tuberculosis is caused by a bacterium that most often attacks the lungs, but it can spread throughout the body. It usually travels from person-to-person through the air and is spread by coughing and sneezing.

It was generally assumed that tuberculosis was brought into western Canada by new European immigrants because the disease reached epidemic levels amongst the First Nations in the late-1800s when there was a high influx of new settlers. However, recent research carried out at Stanford University indicates that the disease entered western Canada from Quebec. It was brought in by the fur trade voyageurs and lay dormant amongst the infected First Nation people until the host environment deteriorated, allowing the disease to develop in the body.[259] The host environment degradation was attributable to the First Nation reserves and the demise of the bison. The creation of the reserves resulted in the First Nation population being required to live in close quarters and in poor housing conditions. The demise of the bison created famine conditions, which greatly decreased proper food supply, which was not augmented by food from other sources nor from the government.

Dr. R.G. Ferguson, a pioneer in the study of tuberculosis, wrote in his report: "With few exceptions, all these plains Indians were reported to be free of anything that would approach an epidemic up to at least 1882. Between 1882 and 1885 for some reason there was a tremendous increase in the frequency of the disease, and at a later date, on practically all the reserves on the plains the disease had taken on the proportions of an epidemic."[260] We now know "for some reason" was malnutrition, over-crowded living conditions, and poorly ventilated housing on the reserves. As Ferguson indicated, the disease was far-reaching. From 1884, the reserve populations declined significantly. For example, the population at Crooked River Reserve declined by 41 percent and that of File Hills reserve decreased by 46 percent. By 1889, less than half of the pre-rebellion population of the Battleford reserves survived.[261]

First Nation children who lived in residential and industrial schools did not escape tuberculosis epidemics. Overcrowding, poor nutrition, and inadequate ventilation resulted in the spread of the disease amongst the children with a resulting high mortality rate. Records show that authorities were aware of the high risks for students who attended the schools. Dr. Seymour reported that: "One of the things to do towards lessening the amount of tuberculosis is to relieve the over-crowding conditions of the school. Additional sleeping and classroom accommodation should be immediately provided." It would appear these recommendations were not carried out. For example, at the Qu'Appelle Industrial School, where there were fewer than 170 students, fifty-two children died.[262]

Just as the government had failed to assist when the bison were dying and famine had struck amongst First Nations, the government did little to assist with the tuberculosis outbreaks even though it had a moral obligation, if not a legal one, to do so. As noted earlier under the terms of Treaty No. 6, the Crown was obligated to assist the First Nations with outbreaks of "pestilence."

Tuberculosis epidemics began occurring within the Inuit populations in the 1900s. It was estimated that at least one-third of all Inuit were infected with TB by the 1950s.[263] By this time, sanatoria had been established for the treatment of the disease in southern Canada. Inuit patients were transported to facilities in such places as Hamilton, Ontario, where one sanatorium treated about 1,200 Inuit patients. Prior to the development of antibiotics, treatment and recovery took weeks and months.

Inuit patients were, for the most part, transported to southern Canada via the Coast Guard ship *C.D. Howe*. Examination of potential patients was made on board the ship while it was anchored in the harbour. Once the doctors decided who needed to go south for treatment in sanatoria or hospitals, they were not allowed to go ashore to collect belongings or say goodbye to family and friends. In some cases, they never saw each other again. In 1956, it was estimated that one-seventh of the entire Inuit population was being treated in southern Canada. The average length of stay was two to three years, with some patients staying longer. Patients were treated poorly by authorities. Some Inuit were identified by number, rather than by name, and they were not permitted to speak in their Inuit language. Many families were not notified when a TB patient died in the south. The dead were buried in poorly identified graves in a southern cemetery with costs paid for by the Department of Northern Affairs.[264]

On March 8, 2019, Prime Minister Justin Trudeau made a formal apology, on behalf of the Government of Canada, for the inadequate health care inflicted on the Inuit people. The apology was made in Iqaluit, where Trudeau called the treatment of the Inuit, an act of "colonialism." He stated: "We are sorry for forcing you from your families, for not showing the respect and care you deserve. We are sorry for your pain." As part of the apology, the government promised to establish a database that would make records available to the Inuit to facilitate finding family-member gravesites.[265] While the apology has been accepted, many Inuit still grieve for family members buried in unknown graves.

Water Quality and Flooding

The issue of safe drinking water in First Nation communities remains a major health concern, continuing to create an extra burden on people's lives. For example, in October 2015, Neskantaga First Nation reported that its twenty-year boiling-water advisory was the longest running advisory on drinking water in Canada. Shoal Lake 40 First Nation was under an eighteen-year boil-water advisory.[266] As of May 31, 2019, there were still fifty-eight long-term drinking water advisories affecting First Nation communities.[267] In the case of the Kashechewan First Nation in northern Ontario, the problem of water quality and flooding has existed since 1976. Some twenty years before, the Cree community was ordered by both the provincial and federal governments to settle on the northern banks of the Albany River near James Bay. Since the 1970s, the community has flooded and has required evacuation seventeen times due to spring snow melts and river flooding. The current community of some 2,500 residents had to be evacuated again in 2019. Even though both the provincial and federal governments have promised to relocate the community to higher ground, no concrete action has taken place so far.[268]

The First Nation of Attawapiskat, 700 kilometres north of Sudbury, Ontario, has been struggling with health and social issues for a number of years. In April 2016, it declared a state of emergency due to an epidemic of suicide attempts on the reserve. Between September 2015 and April 2016, there were over a hundred suicide attempts, most of them children under fourteen, along with many young adults under the age of twenty-five. The health services capacity at the First Nation was overwhelmed with the crisis.[269] In July 2019, the First Nation declared a second state of emergency due to a breakdown in the community's potable water supply. Water tests showed harmful levels of two toxic contaminates, making the water unsuitable for drinking, washing of food, and even bathing. The Minster of Indigenous Services, Seamus O'Regan, visited the community on July 21, 2019, and attended a community meeting. He promised a follow-up with a public health official and an engineering team. No timetable was established.[270]

The Asubpeeschoseewagong (Grassy Narrows) First Nation, along with others, signed Treaty No. 3 in 1871, surrendering to the Crown aboriginal title to a large tract of land in the Dryden area of western Ontario. In exchange, the First Nation received an area of reserve land along the Wabigoon-English River system along with the right to hunt and fish on unused Crown land that had been given up. Included in the Crown's obligations were the establishment of schools and the supply of equipment, implements, and supplies to enable economic development. Upstream from the Wabigoon-English River system, the Dryden Chemical Company and the Dryden Pulp and Paper Companies were established in 1962. Between 1962 and 1970, an estimated ten tons of mercury was discharged into the river, polluting the river and lakes into which the river flowed. As a result, river and lake fish were contaminated with mercury, which poisoned any Asubpeeschoseewagong residents who ate them. The contamination of the fish stock caused the community's fish plant to close and the tourist fishing industry to collapse. Both the provincial and federal governments, while having made promises to deal with the health and economy conditions experienced by the Asubpeeschoseewagong First Nation, have failed to act in a meaningful way. Some fifty years later, the residents continue to suffer mercury poisoning, and there is high unemployment. As the result of the continuing lack of progress, the current Asubpeeschoseewagong chief announced his intention to run in the 2019 federal election, hoping to bring pressure on the federal government to take action.[271, 272]

Child Welfare

Colonialism by neglect with respect to Indigenous children continues today. In a 2019 study titled "Toward Justice: Tackling Indigenous Child Poverty in Canada," it was determined that 47 percent of Status First Nation children in Canada live in poverty, two-and-a-half times the national average. The study found that there has been no improvement in reducing children poverty levels from 2005.[273,274] An example of why progress has not been made in meeting the needs of Indigenous children is the decision made by the federal government to challenge a ruling by the Canadian Human Rights Tribunal that found Canada guilty of: "willfully underfunding on-reserve child welfare and ordered each child be paid $40,000, a settlement that could amount to billions of dollars".[275] The ruling followed the tribunal's decision on January 28, 2016, that found "Canada guilty of purposefully discriminating against First Nations Children."[276] The decision to challenge the tribunal's ruling was made even though Indigenous Services Minister Seamus O'Regan stated: "We agree with the many findings of the Canadian Human Rights Tribunal, including the recognition of discrimination and mistreatment and the need for compensation."[277]

Social Services

Another example of continuing colonialism by neglect has been identified in the province of Quebec with the release of Justice Vien's report, which documented how Indigenous Peoples are treated by police, the province's youth protection agency, health and social services, as well as the justice and correctional systems. In his report, Viens stated: "It seems impossible to deny the systematic discrimination experienced by First Nation and Inuit peoples in their relationship with the public services investigated."[278] Ghislain Picard, Chief of the Assembly of First Nations for Quebec and Labrador stated: "We have before us a two-tier system. The one that must meet the expectations and needs of First Nations is sorely lacking. The current system discriminates against our peoples and makes them second-class citizens."[279] Quebec premier, Francois Legault, on October 2, 2019, formally apologized to the Indigenous Peoples in Quebec: "As a result,

I offer members of the First Nations and the Inuit in Quebec the most sincere apology from the whole Quebec state…The Quebec state failed in its duty to you. …We need to understand the reasons which brought us to this situation … and we must change things."[280] However, the government did not offer any immediate action.

Chapter 8

Colonialism by Embedded Racism

THE PRACTICES OF RACISM AND COLONIALISM ARE INTERTWINED AND feed on one another. Racism is generally demonstrated by the display of presumed superiority while colonialism is generally demonstrated by the enactment of superiority. In some cases, however, such as in law enforcement, when police arbitrarily stop and arrest Black or Indigenous Canadians, it is a combination of both. This chapter will deal with the treatment of Black Canadians, First Nations, Metis and Inuit, and Chinese Canadians as to the practice of racism and colonialism in Canada.

Black Canadians

The prejudice against people of colour in North America, especially Black people, has a long and difficult history. In Canada, while Black people only make up about 3 percent of the population, in some parts of the country, they make up 33 percent of those killed by police. Black Canadians are incarcerated in federal prisons at a rate three times higher than the proportion of Blacks in the general population.[281]

Slavery and the Origins of Racist Attitudes

The origins of prejudice against Black Canadians begin with the slavery of peoples of Africa. The first African slave captured and transferred out of the African continent occurred in 1444. It is estimated that between 1444 and the 1880s, approximately 15 million Africans were bound, chained, and forced to leave the African continent against their will. In addition, many Africans died within the continent while walking from their homes in the interior of the continent to the West African shores for boarding onto slave ships. Added to that total were those who died on board ships that took them across the Atlantic Ocean to Caribbean countries and to North and South America.[282]

While the majority of slaves were taken by European landholders to the Caribbean to work on sugar-cane farms and by American cotton plantation owners, some were taken by French colonizers to Atlantic Canada. There are two accounts about the first Black slaves to enter Canada. The first identifies Mathew Da Costa as entering Canada in Nova Scotia in 1606. He reportedly arrived with explorer Pierre Du Gua De Monts.[283] The second was Oliver Le Jeune, who entered the country in 1628.[284] The New France settler colonies located in Ile Royale, now called Cape Breton Island, bought both Black and Indigenous slaves to work, unpaid, in the building of their farms and other enterprises. "New France's colonists supported slavery for many reasons: to make up for lagging profits in the fur trade, to try to replicate the wealth they had seen in the slave economies of the West Indies, and as a means of obtaining free labour for domestic and agricultural work."[285]

Slavery in New France was sanctioned by King Louis XIV in 1689 when he gave royal assent to requests from France's colonies, including those in Canada, to legalize the practice. Slaveholding was widespread in New France, practised by government officials, judges, business owners, landlords, notaries, doctors, military officials, clergy, religious orders, and hospitals. The sale of slaves was public, inhuman, and degrading: "It was not uncommon for Black and Indigenous people to be sold side-by-side with livestock, at slave auctions and in the newspaper."[286]

The laws concerning slavery in Atlantic Canada did not change with the British victory over France in the Seven Years War. Under the Treaty of Paris in 1763, France was required to surrender control of its colonies in Canada to the British. However, existing slave owners retained their rights to their human chattel. The practice of Black enslavement was expanded under British rule in Canada. This was particularly true as British colonizers expanded within what is now Nova Scotia and beyond. English-speaking Upper Canada (present-day southern Ontario) became a slave-owning colony. French-speaking Lower Canada (present-day Quebec) continued the practice of slavery that had started under French rule.

While abolition of slavery by the British government occurred in 1834, resulting in the same status for Canada, but the institutionalized prejudice against Black peoples in Canada and elsewhere was already deeply embedded. Black individuals, particularly of African descent, were to be treated differently—as people to be feared and not trusted. As an example, in 1910, almost eighty years after abolition, the Edmonton Board of Trade launched a petition to stop Black immigration to Canada, based on their observation and belief that the experience in the United States showed that "negroes and white cannot live in proximity without the occurrence of revolting lawlessness and the development of bitter race hatred."[287] One year later, in 1911, the Canadian federal government passed an Order-in-Council prohibiting "immigrants belonging to the Negro race, which race is deemed unsuitable to the climate and requirements in Canada." The federal government went so far as to send agents to Oklahoma to specifically discourage African Americans from considering moving north to Canada.[288]

Following the Second World War and the atrocities and prejudices shown against certain races, the Canadian government decided to reduce its discriminatory policies, but only up to a point. Prime Minister Mackenzie King outlined Canada's policy in a speech to the House of Commons in 1950: "The policy of the government is to foster the growth of population in Canada by encouraging immigration. The government will seek, through legislation, regulation and vigorous administration, to ensure the careful selection and permanent settlement of such members of immigrants as can advantageously be absorbed into our national economy.... With regard to the selection of immigrants much has been said about discrimination, I wish to make it quite clear Canada is perfectly within her rights in selecting persons whom we regard as desirable future citizens. It is not a 'fundamental human right' of any alien to enter Canada. It is a privilege. It is a matter of domestic policy.... There will, I am sure, be general agreement with the view that the people of Canada do not wish, as a result of mass immigration, to make a fundamental alteration in the character of our population."[289] The latter statement has been interpreted that the intent was to keep Canada predominantly white.

While race was not mentioned in the new policy, the policy was interpreted by government officials to identify who was admissible into Canada. For example, an immigration officer in a memo to a fellow officer wrote: "It is not by accident that coloured British subjects other than negligible members from the United Kingdom are excluded from Canada.... They do not assimilate readily and pretty much vegetate to a low standard of living. Despite what has been said to the contrary, many cannot adapt themselves to our climate conditions."[290] It was not until the 1960s that Canada started to change its racist attitude, allowing Blacks to enter Canada on the same basis as other immigrants. Yet, there were lingering biases against Black immigrants. In the case of immigrants from Caribbean countries who were hired as domestic workers in Canada, the Deputy Minister of Citizenship and Immigration stated in 1964: "One single female domestic servant may take a year or two to become established, but she may then begin to sponsor brothers, sisters, fiancé and parents at a fairly rapid rate. The one unsponsored worker may meet someone's need for a domestic servant for a year or two, but the result may be ten or twenty sponsored immigrants of dubious value to Canada and who may well cause insoluble social problems.... I am greatly concerned that we may be facing a West Indian sponsorship explosion."[291]

Education – Black Canadians

The settlement of African Americans in Canada occurred in two main areas. The first was in Atlantic Canada by Loyalists who brought their slaves with them when they moved to Canada and slaves who won their freedom through their allegiance to Britain during the American War of Independence. The second settlement was in southern Ontario, by runaway slaves and others using the network of secret routes known as the Underground Railroad. It is estimated that approximately 5,500 migrants initially settled in Nova Scotia and New Brunswick, and by the time of the American Civil War an estimated 30,000 fugitives settled in Southern Ontario.[292]

The education of Black Canadians in the Canadian school systems has a history distinct from the education of white Canadians. With the influx of Black immigrants into Canada from the United States in the eighteenth and nineteenth centuries, the provinces of Nova Scotia and Ontario created legally segregated public-school systems for Black children.

In the early years, British charitable organizations sponsored schools in most of the Maritime Black communities, and British and American societies established schools for Blacks in Ontario. This was possible because the Black immigrants were forced to settle in segregated communities, usually on the outskirts of large white towns. When the provincial governments took over operating the segregated schools, they were underfunded and provided an inferior level of instruction compared to the regular white schools. The last segregated school in Ontario was closed in 1965; the last segregated school in Nova Scotia was closed in 1983. Affected students, however, were now required to spend considerable time on buses to attend integrated schools, usually long distances from their homes. In addition, even in some integrated schools, Black students were required to use separate entrances and washrooms, as late as the 1960s.[293]

The legacy of the segregated schools and substandard education provided to Black students was still evident in the 1960s. For example, a survey conducted in 1962 by the Institute of Public Affairs in Nova Scotia found that most Black adults had education levels between grades four and nine. In Nova Scotia in 1969, only 3 percent of Black students graduated from high school and only 1 percent of the graduates attended university.[294]

In her book *Policing Black Lives,* Robyn Maynard postulates that, even today, Black students are excessively streamed into individual program plans that are unsuitable or not required.[295] Maynard also suggests that Black youth are often treated as "suspects instead of as the children they are." This suspicion and mistrust of Black students by teachers often manifests itself in expulsion from school. For example, in Toronto, between 2011-2012 and 2015-2016, almost half of the students expelled from the Toronto District School Board were Black, while only 10 percent of those expelled were white. In Halifax, during the 2015-2016 school year, Black students made up 8 percent of the student population, but they made up 22.5 percent of total suspensions.[296]

There has been an improvement in the numbers of Black students completing grade 12 in recent years. For example, according to the 2006 Canadian Census, Black Canadian education and language skill levels were not too dissimilar from those of all visible minorities and the total Canadian population.[297] However, Black students continue to have higher-than-average school drop-out rates. For example, for the 2006 to 2011 period, the Toronto School Board found that, overall, Black students had the lowest graduation rate of any group, at 65 percent.[298] Black students still continue to experience the stress of "being different" and being subject to overt and subtle discrimination by staff and students.

Blacks and the Canadian Labour Market

In comparison with other Canadians, including other visible minorities, Blacks have a higher unemployment rate and are more likely to work in lower-paying jobs. According to the 2006 Canadian Census, Black Canadians in the workforce had an unemployment rate of 10.7 percent in comparison with that for all visible minorities of 8.6 percent and for all Canadians at 6.6 percent. The situation has not improved. According to the 2016 Census, the Black unemployment rate increased to 12.5 percent, while the total Canadian rate was 7.7 percent. By occupation, Blacks are under-represented in management positions and in the fields of art, culture, recreation, and sports and over-represented in lower-paying positions such as health services. In 2005, for example, the average yearly income for Black Canadians was $27,143, compared to $27,786 for all visible minorities and $35,498 for all Canadians.[299]

Direct discrimination and racism are thought to be two factors that contribute to Black underachievement in the labour market. As Joseph Mensah points out in his book *Black Canadians,* related macro-level factors, such as class, culture, education, and province of residency may also interact with these.[300]

Racial Profiling and Treatment

Racial profiling of Blacks and other visible minorities by police has been and continues to be an ongoing concern in Canada. A number of studies have been undertaken to examine the issue, and cases concerning racial profiling have reached Canada's courts.

The most widely accepted definition of racial profiling was the one put forward by the Supreme Court in a case that was before it in 1999. The court defined racial profiling as "criminal profiling based on race. Racial or colour profiling refers to that phenomenon whereby certain criminal activity is attributed to an identified group in society based on race or colour resulting in the targeting of individual members of that group. In this context, the race is illegitimately used as a proxy for the criminality or general criminal propensity of an entire racial group."[301]

An example of racial profiling that occurred in 2001 was brought before the Ontario Superior Court. In this case, two young African Canadian men and two young women were stopped and searched in an alleyway by an undercover police officer. The officer indicated, while giving testimony, that race and other factors such as location were the basis for suspicion. In finding that race of the accused was a significant factor in the officer's decision to stop them for questioning, the court determined that "there was neither a basis for investigative detention nor reasonable grounds to suspect criminal activity. They found that race—especially the race of a young male—either alone or in the context of facts, does not provide reasonable grounds for suspecting criminal activity. The court concluded that stereotypical assumptions linking young Black men and the use of narcotics do not provide a lawful basis to detain or arrest them."[302] In a case before the Supreme Court, also in 2001, the court suggested that minority groups in Canada are over-policed and that Charter of Rights standards must be developed to "reduce the danger of racist stereotyping by individual police officers."[303]

In 2002, the *Toronto Star* newspaper reported that Black Torontonians were overrepresented in certain charge categories and that Black offenders were treated more harshly following street arrest and were much more likely to be held in custody for bail hearings than their white counterparts. The *Star* contended that these patterns were upheld even when other relevant legal factors had been taken into account.[304] Another study conducted by criminologist Scott Wortley at the University of Toronto found that Black people were four times more likely to be pulled over by police and that 40 percent of Black males between the ages of fifteen and twenty-four were stopped by police during the study year, compared to 11 percent of their white counterparts.[305]

Profiles on Blacks and others are obtained by police by a practice known as "carding." Information gathered at the time someone is stopped by the police for questioning is recorded on cards and then filed. The *Toronto Star*, by means of Access to Information requests, found that in Toronto, between 2008 and 2011, 1.25 million contact cards were filled out by police, and nearly one-quarter of those documented were Black. Findings showed that young Blacks were carded at a rate 3.4 times higher that of the general population, and these rates were even higher for Black people stopped in predominantly white neighbourhoods.[306] Similar research carried out by the Canadian Broadcasting Corporation in Halifax in 2017 showed that Blacks were checked by police at a rate 3.1 times higher than white people. Ashley Taylor, a student support worker at Dartmouth High School, reported that he is stopped on average three times a year, usually on his way to work.[307]

Black Canadians, besides having a greater chance of being arbitrarily stopped for questioning by police, are also at a greater risk of physical attack by police. According to a 2018 interim report prepared by the Ontario Human Rights Commission, Black people are more likely than white people to be injured or killed by Toronto Police. The commission analyzed hundreds of previously inaccessible reports completed by Ontario's Special Investigations Unit for the periods 2000 and 2006, 2013, and 2017. The report indicated that while Blacks made up only 8.8 percent of Toronto's population in 2016, they were involved in seven out of ten cases of fatal shootings by police in the 2013 to 2017 period.[308,309]

The findings of a 2019 study carried out by Scott Wortley, a criminology professor at the University of Toronto, showed that street checks of Black persons in Halifax have increased in recent years rather than decreased. The report on racial profiling by Halifax-area police found that Black people were street checked at a rate six times higher than that of white people. In a similar study carried out two years earlier, the rate for street checks of Black people was three times higher than of white people. The study also found that police in the Halifax region do more street checks than police in Montreal, Vancouver, or Ottawa.[310]

The over-policing of Black Canadians has both short- and long-term negative consequences for the individuals affected and on their families. Robin Maynard, citing research from the Ontario Human Rights Commission Report "Paying the Price: The Human Cost of Racial Profiling,"[311] indicates that the stress experienced can cause post-traumatic stress disorder, other stress disorders, and alienation. One mother, cited in the 2003 Ontario Human Rights Commission report:[312] said, "Now I am very afraid for my two boys. I'm afraid for them to go out. I can't sleep when they go out. I'm scared when they go out with Black friends. They're like a magnet. It's not fair that four Black kids can't walk around."[313]

Indigenous Peoples - First Nations, Inuit, and Metis

Violence against Women

In a 2004 report, Amnesty International found that Status Indian women in Canada between the ages of twenty-five and forty-four were five times more likely than other Canadian women to die as a result of violence.[314] A 2010 report "What Their Stories Tell Us: Research Findings from the Sisters in Spirit Initiative," which was carried out by the Native Women's Association of Canada, postulates that there is a direct link between violence against Aboriginal women and the history of colonialism, present-day racism, and the socio-economic marginalization of Aboriginal women. The report states: "The experience of violence and victimization of Aboriginal women does not occur in a vacuum. Violence is perpetuated through apathy and indifference toward Aboriginal women, and stems from the ongoing impacts of colonialism in Canada. While the process is rooted in history, the impacts of colonialism continue to effect Aboriginal peoples, and perhaps more profoundly Aboriginal women today. Systematic racism and patriarchy have marginalized Aboriginal women and led to intersecting issues of colonialism in a climate where Aboriginal women are particularly vulnerable to violence, victimization and indifference by the state and society."[315]

Statistics Canada, in its 2014 Homicide Report, found that Indigenous women were six times more likely to be the victim of a homicide than non-Indigenous women. The RCMP, in their report "Missing and Murdered Aboriginal Women: A National Operational Overview" released in 2014, found 1,017 police-recorded incidents of Indigenous female homicides between 1980 and 2012. They also found 164 cases of missing Indigenous females between 1951 and 2012.[316]

In 2016, the Canadian government established a National Inquiry into Missing and Murdered Indigenous Women and Girls. The inquiry's format included statement gatherings, expert and knowledge keeper's hearings, and Indigenous law and human rights hearings. Its report was released on June 3, 2019. The inquiry found that Indigenous women and girls are twelve times more likely to be murdered or go missing than members of any other demographic group in Canada and sixteen times more likely to be slain or to disappear than white women. The inquiry also found that Indigenous women and girls made up almost 25 percent of all female homicide victims in Canada between 2001 and 2015. As summarized by the CBC, the Inquiry report found that often, murder investigations are "marked by indifference" and negative stereotypes that result in Indigenous deaths and disappearance being investigated and treated differently from other cases—differences that result in fewer solved cases.[317] In one of its conclusions, the Inquiry report stated: "This genocide has been empowered by colonial structures, evidenced notably by the Indian Act, the Sixties Scoop, Residential Schools and breaches of human and Indigenous rights, leading directly to the current increase rates of violence, deaths and suicide in the Indigenous populations."[318]

The inquiry heard from over 2,000 people during its investigations. The following are two examples of what they heard, as reported during the media release:

- "My daughter Hillary went missing on September 15, 2009," said Pamela Filler from Esgenoopetitj First Nation in New Brunswick.

"When I went to the police, they assumed she was out partying and did not look for her."[319]

- Melanie Morrison, a Mohawk Mi'gmaq women in Quebec, said her sister went missing June 18, 2006. "It was unlike my sister to not come home because she was a young mother. When my mom went to the police, she was met with the stereotype that because she was only twenty-four, she was probably just out with friends and would show up. Unfortunately, my sister's remains were found four years later. It was devastating because where she was found was less than a kilometre from her home."[320]

Forced Sterilization

The sterilization of Indigenous women without their consent had been reported for a number of years. According to Dr. Karen Stote at Wilfrid Laurier University, between 1971 and 1974: "At least 580 sterilizations took place at federally operated hospitals in the prairie provinces, Yukon, N.W.T. and Ontario with Indigenous women making up 95 per cent of those sterilizations."[321] More recently, the Saskatchewan Health Authority apologized in 2017 for their role in forced sterilization on First Nations women, and admitted they had "much work to do" in addressing related systematic issues.[322] The Saskatchewan case has developed into a proposed class-action law suit against the Health Authority, the Province of Saskatchewan, the Government of Canada, as well as the physicians involved. According to the lawyers involved, reports on involuntary cases of sterilization are coming from the NWT, Yukon, Manitoba, Ontario, Alberta, and BC.[323]

There is now new evidence that suggests that this practice may be continuing. On June 18, 2019, RCMP Commissioner Brenda Lucki requested victims of forced sterilization to contact the RCMP in their province or territory.[324] In addition, on August 7, 2019, the House of Commons Health Committee asked the government to investigate the continuing forced sterilization of women in Canada after it heard evidence of a case of sterilization without consent that took place in December 2018 at a hospital in Moose Jaw, Saskatchewan.[325]

The Metis People

The existence of Metis people in Canada goes back hundreds of years, but it was not until 1982 that they were identified, under Section 35 of the Constitution Act 1982, as one of the three Aboriginal Peoples of Canada; the other two were the First Nation and Inuit peoples. Over the years, successive federal and provincial governments have avoided recognizing their existence as an organized group and that the government held any meaningful obligation to them. It is only through the courts in such cases as R v Powley (Metis hunting rights); MMF v Canada (Manitoba Act): and Daniels v. Canada (federal, not provincial responsibility) that Canada's obligation to the Metis Peoples have been recognized.[326]

Generally, Metis are Canadians identified of mixed European and Indigenous ancestry, although there has been, and continues to be, controversy over an exact definition and agreement on ancestral roots, including place of original residence. The complexity of agreeing on exactly who qualifies to be a Metis in Canada is addressed by Jean Teillet in her book *The North-West is Our Mother.*[327] According to the 2016 Canadian Census, the Metis population in Canada is 587,545, although Statistics Canada has placed a caveat on this number because of the confusion of self-identification on the census form and the question as to who qualifies as a Metis person.[328]

Prior to the nineteenth century, Canada's Metis were generally occupied as voyageurs, fur traders, transporters, food suppliers, and as employees of the Hudson's Bay Company and the North West Company. At the beginning of the 1800s, many started to settle in the Red River region of what is now Winnipeg and environs. As their population grew, so did the population of other settlers, such as the Selkirk Settlers as promoted by Lord Selkirk. And, as both populations grew, so did the conflict between the Metis and the non-Indigenous Peoples. The conflict was further stoked by members of the pro-British Orange Lodge located in Ontario, who wanted to see the area under the control of the British-oriented population.

The Red River region, at the time of Canada's confederation in 1867, was known as Rupert's Land and was under the control of the Hudson's Bay Company. In 1869, the newly formed Dominion of Canada and the Hudson's Bay Company reached an agreement for the transfer of Rupert's

Land to the Canadian government. It was estimated that the total population in the Red River region in 1870 was 12,000, of which 85 percent were Metis, almost equally divided between French and English speakers.[329] Given the large Metis population and its history in the region, the Metis, both French and English, under the leadership of Louis Riel, wanted to establish a Metis nation in the Red River region as a part of Canada. Riel and his followers petitioned the government in Ottawa to hear their request.

Ignoring the Metis request to meet, the Canadian government proceeded to survey the land in section squares, generally ignoring established Metis occupied parcels of land. The result was armed conflict, known as the Red River Resistance, between the Metis population and government officials, including the military. To better organize their efforts, the Metis established the Metis National Committee.

The Metis National Committee, working with French and English Metis as well as other Indigenous and non-Indigenous Peoples, formed the Provisional Government of Assiniboia's Legislative Assembly. In March 1870, the provisional government sent a delegation to Ottawa to negotiate Red River's entrance into Confederation. The result of the meetings was the proclamation of the Manitoba Act that established Manitoba as a province of Canada.[330]

The Manitoba Act had a number of provisions that were of direct interest to the Metis. It allocated 1,400,000 acres of land for them. English and French language rights were safeguarded in the new legislature and the courts, as were certain Protestant and Catholic educational rights. The Act did not address the issue of a Metis nation and retained federal control over Manitoba's natural resources and all unallocated land.[331] Unfortunately, any victories the Metis thought they had achieved were short-lived as the federal government's colonial instinct took hold and a number of the agreements were left unfulfilled. For example, only some 15 percent of the original 1.4 million acres promised under the Act were ever distributed. In addition, most of the bilingual right given to Manitobans were later abolished.[332]

To avoid allocating land to the Metis as a group, as was noted in Chapter 6, the government used scrip as a vehicle for transferring land to individual Metis. But by procrastinating in implementing the scrip system, the government, by and large, avoided transferring land to both individuals and communities. According to The Canadian Encyclopedia, the "Metis scrip was a document, either a certificate or warrant, issued by the Department of the Interior and printed by the Canadian Bank Note Company. It came in two forms: money scrip in increments of $20, $80, $120 and $240, and land scrip, issued in land allotments of 80, 160 and 240 acres."[333] The distribution of the scrip to the Metis was complex and cumbersome as was the redemption of the scrips. In addition, fraudsters and speculators entered the process with the result that very little land was actually transferred to the Metis.[334]

A large number of Red River Metis became disappointed with the outcome of their desires within Manitoba. Their livelihood and preferred way of life were threatened. As a result, many moved farther west into what are now Alberta and Saskatchewan. The history of those who settled in Saskatchewan near St. Laurent, Duck Lake, and Batoche on the South Saskatchewan River has been described in Chapter 6.

The Mysterious Killing of Inuit Sled Dogs by the RCMP and Others

From the 1950s to the 1970s, the Royal Canadian Mounted Police and the Quebec Provincial Police killed an estimated 20,000 Inuit sled dogs, rendering the breed extinct.[335] The dogs were used by the Inuit for hundreds of years as their chief means of transportation in the winter months, as well as to help hunting parties find seal's breathing holes in the ice and to recall routes to safety during heavy snow storms. The exact reasons for the killings remain a mystery and are controversial. The Inuit saw the killing of the dogs as part of the Canadian government's systematic effort to force Inuit into year-round settlements and abandon their semi-nomadic way of life. This was in addition to other government policies, such as forced relocations, residential schools, and welfare payments that were intended to force the Inuit to live in permanent settlements.[336] Without dogs, the Inuit could not travel and had to abandon winter homes, trap lines, hunting grounds, and ice-fishing spots.

The reason for killing the sled dogs has been investigated. The RCMP carried out an internal investigation in 2005, but they announced that they had found no evidence of any conspiracy to kill the dogs. Between 2007 and 2010, the Qikiqtani Truth Commission did an investigation and reported that they found no evidence of a conspiracy to shoot the dogs.[337] There has been no argument that the dogs were shot, but the reason for the dogs extinction remains undetermined. In the meantime, Carolyn Bennett, Minister of Crown-Indigenous Relations, on August 14, 2019, issued an apology for the killing of the Inuit dogs. She is quoted as stating: "The government made a mistake by assuming it knew best for Inuit people. We have and will learn from these great errors".[338] In 2011, the Quebec government signed an agreement with Nunavik's Makivik Corp. to pay $3 million to the Inuit to support the protection and promotion of their culture as compensation for the killing of their dogs.[339] Regardless of formal responsibility, the insult and consequences to the Inuit people is real. In 2005, Lucien Ukalianuk, one of the people affected, stated: "We went to Iglulik in a boat and let our dogs off first. They were roaming free. The next thing we knew, they were all shot. The police purposely went out to shoot dogs, everybody's dog. The government and the police were the law. They could do whatever they wanted." [340]

The Chinese Head Tax and the Chinese Exclusion Act

Perhaps the most overt act of racism and its colonial application that has been carried out by the Canadian government was the imposition of the Chinese head tax and the introduction of the Chinese Exclusion Act. The Chinese head tax was levied on Chinese immigrants between 1885 and 1923 under the Chinese Immigration Act (1885). The Chinese Exclusion Act was passed by the Canadian government in 1923. It prohibited any Chinese immigration to Canada, until it was repealed in 1947.

Initial immigration to Canada by the Chinese started around 1858, but the bulk of it occurred from 1881 to 1885. It is estimated that some 15,000 Chinese labourers came to Canada to work on the construction of the trans-Canada Canadian Pacific Railway. At the completion of the railway construction in 1885, the Chinese labourers sought other employment. However, trade unionists, certain politicians, and others in British Columbia began agitating against the new immigrants. As a consequence, the federal government established a Royal Commission on Chinese Immigration to investigate allegations against the Chinese. In 1885, the commission concluded that there was little evidence to support negative claims against the Chinese and that Chinese immigration was, in fact, beneficial to the economic development of British Columbia. However, the government bowed to political and societal pressure and enacted the Chinese Immigration Act that included a $50 head tax to be imposed on any new immigrants from China. A typical labourer at that time earned about $300 a year, so the tax was a significant monetary penalty.

Notwithstanding the tax, Chinese immigration continued, resulting in a second inquiry being established. The Royal Commission on Chinese and Japanese Immigration recommended that the head tax be increased to $500. This new tax, enacted by parliament in 1903, was equivalent to approximately a two-year salary. While immigration at that time to Canada from Europe and the United States was promoted with incentives, the Chinese were the only people upon whom a head tax was imposed to discourage immigration.

During the years of the head tax, from 1885 to 1923, an estimated 82,000 Chinese immigrants paid nearly $23 million in tax.[341] But despite the taxes and other disincentive restrictions, Chinese immigration to Canada persisted. To counteract this, the government, in 1923, passed the Chinese Exclusion Act that banned all Chinese immigrants except for some business persons, diplomats, and students. This act stayed in force for twenty-four years, until it was repealed in 1947.

Chinese Canadians who immigrated to Canada before 1923 and even after 1947 were subjected to institutional racism and internal colonialism. The Chinese Immigration Act required them to pay a head tax, and they were treated as second-class citizens. They were denied the right to vote, to practice law or medicine, to hold public office, to serve in the military, and to work on public works projects or on Crown land. At the same time, the government took advantage of those Chinese Canadian men who felt Canada to be their home by asking them to serve in the army in highly dangerous situations during the later stages of World War II. They were assigned to serve with the British army in southeast Asia where they worked in a secret service branch behind enemy lines to carry out dangerous demolition and spying activities.[342]

The Chinese Canadian community suffered in public esteem for many years until the prejudicial attitudes of government and certain elements of society began to change their views. The community, through a number of organizations and over a number of years, attempted to obtain an apology from the Canadian government and some form of redress for the events that had occurred. In 2005, Prime Minister Paul Martin made a personal apology, which was not accepted by the Chinese community as sufficient. On June 22, 2006, newly elected Prime Minister Stephen Harper apologized in the House of Commons to head-tax payers, their families, and the Chinese Canadian community. He pledged symbolic payments to living head-tax payers and living spouses of deceased payers.[343] A commitment was also made to establish funds to help finance community projects aimed at acknowledging the impact of past wartime measures and immigration restrictions. Some 785 people were reported to have received $20,000 each from the federal government. The premiers of Newfoundland and British Columbia also made apologies with respect to legislation targeting Chinese Canadians in their provinces.

Chapter 9

Hidden Internal Colonialism within the Military, Police Forces, and Public Services

USING THE DEFINITION OF COLONIALISM "AS THE PRACTICE OF DOMINATION, which involves the subjugation of one people to another" cited earlier in this book, there are a number of instances of colonialism that remain hidden from view and that may continue to be practised in Canada. They tend to be highly personal with those affected keeping a low profile, but they have a hurt that runs deep and lasts for many years.

LGBTQ Canadians in Public Service

One case of internal colonialism in Canada is the treatment of lesbian, gay, bisexual and transgender (LGBT) Canadians in the military, the RCMP, and in the public service. The first criminal trial for homosexuality in the military in Canada occurred in New France in 1648 when a military drummer was sentenced to death for sodomy. The drummer's sentence was later commuted when he agreed to accept the position of New France's first permanent executioner.[344] During the British North America period, "numerous men were convicted and sentenced to death for sodomy," but none were ever executed in Canada.[345]

In the early 1950s in Canada, with the Cold War increasing in importance, the Canadian Criminal code was amended to brand gay men as "criminal sexual psychopaths" and "dangerous sexual offenders." Once the legislation was passed, a special unit of the RCMP began a campaign aimed at removing gay and lesbian members from the military, government institutions, and the RCMP itself. The campaign was driven by the notion that the "character weakness" of homosexual employees would make them susceptible to blackmail by the Soviet Union. The campaign lasted some thirty years, ending in the 1990s. There were no known cases of gay public or military employees passing information to any foreign power.[346]

According to lawyer Doug Elliot, who led a class-action suit against the government on behalf of the victims of the purges: "These people were damaged by their experience, and very mistrustful. Even the very well-adjusted ones live in a state of barely contained anxiety that something terrible is about to happen to them, particularly in the employment context. A lot of them fear that they're going to show up for work, and they're going to be fired."[347] In 2017, the government settled the class-action suit, agreeing to a payment of up to 110 million dollars to the victims. In a speech in the House of Commons on November 28, 2017, Prime Minister Justin Trudeau issued an apology "for Canada's role in the systemic oppression, criminalization and violence against sexual minorities".[348]

Women in Public Service

Another case of hidden colonialism deals with the treatment of women as officers within the RCMP and female civilian employees working for the force. Sexual and psychological harassment of women within the organization was known inside the organization for many years, but usually through intimidation of the victim, the public was shielded from this knowledge. In 2011, former RCMP Corporal Catherine Galliford made her allegations of sexual harassment public. She was followed by others, including former Constable Janet Merlo, former Inspector Linda Davidson, former Mountie Krista Carle, and former Officer Marge Hudson.[349]

A number of lawsuits claiming sexual assault and harassment against the RCMP were brought forward by members and former members after the extent of the problem became publicly known. As a result, on October 6, 2016, RCMP Commissioner Bob Paulson acknowledged the problem and made a formal apology: "For many of our women, this discrimination and harassment has hurt them mentally and physically. You came to the RCMP wanting to contribute to your community and we failed you. We hurt you. For that, I'm truly sorry."[350] Along with the apology, the RCMP established an initial fund of $100 million for payouts to current and former female officers who were subject to sexual harassment and discrimination. It is estimated that 2,400 claims will be made for compensation.[351] A second sexual harassment and discrimination case against the RCMP affecting women working for the force has been settled out of court. In this instance, the women involved were civilian employees, working in non-policing roles. The settlement, announced on July 8, 2019, is for $100 million, is similar to the agreement reached with the female RCMP officers. Compensation for proven claims that can date back forty-five years could range from $10,000 to $222,000. No formal apology accompanied the settlement agreement, but through the negotiations, it was taken to mean an "acknowledgement of the pain experienced by women who were subjected to harassment and sexual assault while working or volunteering with the RCMP."[352]

Members of the Canadian Armed Forces and employees of the Department of National Defence, both male and female, have, over the years, launched a number of class-action lawsuits for sexual harassment, sexual assault, and discrimination based on sex, gender identity, or sexual orientation. On July 18, 2019, the federal government set aside $900M to settle these claims, pending approval by the courts. While the lawsuits identify evidence of sexual misconduct and the money has been set aside, the government is refusing to admit wrongdoing, even though Defence Minister Harjit Saijan in a statement said: "We know it takes a lot of courage to come forward and share difficult and painful experience and press for change."[353]

Health and Well-Being of Military

Another case of hidden colonialism involves the mandated use of an anti-malaria drug by soldiers active in malaria-prone countries. The drug, mefloquine, is highly effective against malaria and was given to Canadian troops on missions to Somalia, Rwanda, and Afghanistan. Returned veterans are claiming that they, have suffered mental health side effects such as psychosis, rage, paranoia, insomnia and thoughts of suicide from having been made to take the drug. Lawyer Paul Millar, representing some of the veterans' claims that they were forced to take the drug, said: "They were under fear of court martial and imprisonment if they didn't take it. There was fraudulent concealment of the side effects and they were never told that if you suffer certain side affects you need to discontinue the medication."[354] The drug company's own warning label cautions about the potential for serious side effects that can last for years. It is reported that some 1,000 Canadian veterans are joining in lawsuits against the government resulting from the use of the drug.[355] It has been suggested, but not substantiated, that the Canadian soldiers involved in the killing of a Somalian boy during their mission to that country may have been affected by the use of the drug.

Section 4

Conclusion

Chapter 10
Canadian Colonialism: Past and Present

MORE THAN THIRTY INSTANCES OF INTERNAL COLONIALISM, ACHIEVED through forced uprooting and displacement, direct attack and subjugation, disdain, disrespect, and denial of rights, and embedded racism, are discussed in this book. They were carried out by government action and inaction, through government agencies, such as the police and militia, and by other institutions and organizations, usually with government funding. Starting with the Chilcotin War in 1864 to the present, this book has illustrated how internal colonialism has been practised pervasively in Canada. The legacy of past events continues to affect people's lives negatively. What has changed and what does the future hold?

Canadians are just beginning to listen to those affected by internal colonialism. We are somewhat willing to talk about the fact that Canada's Indigenous Peoples have been treated as second-class citizens, and we can see how non-white peoples from Africa, Asia, and the Caribbean and even white immigrants from Eastern Europe have been discriminated against and treated as criminals without justification.

At the same time, mainstream white Canadian society continues to treat Canadian citizens of colour differently from white citizens. Moreover, the Canadian population, in general, is not knowledgeable about Canada's colonial history. For many years, school curricula focused on European history. We were taught to be proud of the fact that the "sun never sets on the British Empire." We were never told about the internment of Canadian citizens during World Wars I and II or about the forced relocation of Quebec Inuit to the High Artic. We were never told about Canada's treaties with the Indigenous Peoples who occupied the lands we presently live on or about Indian Residential Schools and the hurt they inflicted on young First Nations children. According to historian J. P. Millar: "Most Canadians do not believe their government's policies dealing with Aboriginal people have been misguided or pernicious."[356] In his book *Residential Schools and Reconciliation,* Miller references a 2015 survey conducted by the Leger marketing research firm that found 83 percent of respondents agreed or strongly agreed with the statement: "I am proud of the history of Canada."[357] Until more Canadians are aware of our history, shedding our colonial past will continue to occur at a slow pace.

In about one-third of the occurrences documented in this book, governments, either federal or provincial, admitted that they did wrong and offered apologies and, in some cases, financial payment to those adversely affected. However, in most cases where apologies and compensation were made, it was the result of court action brought against governments or by strong lobbying by community organizations. In other words, recognition of colonial behaviour was only admitted when perpetrators were required to do so by the courts or by political expediency—not by voluntary acknowledgement of wrongdoing.

Colonialism and Canada's Indigenous Peoples

How can Indigenous Peoples become free of the burden of continuing colonialism? According to Sid Fiddler, formerly with the First Nations University and former Chief of the Waterhen First Nation, the answer is to use the courts to provide a level of fairness.[358] There are a number of examples to back this belief.

In 2014, twenty-one First Nations who had signed the Robinson-Huron Treaty in 1850 asked the court to examine the current fairness of the $4 annual payment to members stipulated under the treaty. The court found that the Crown has "a mandatory and reviewable obligation" to increase the annual payment "when economic circumstances warrant."[359,360] Justice Patricia Hennessy wrote: "The Treaties were not meant to be the last word on the relationship. Renewal of the relationship was necessary to ensure that both parties could continue to thrive in changing environments."[361]

In another case brought before the court, members of the Lake St. Martin, Dauphin River, Little Saskatchewan, and Pinaymootang First Nations in northern Manitoba received a judge-approved settlement from the federal and provincial governments for flood damage to their communities. During flooding in Manitoba in 2011, the Manitoba government diverted water from the Assiniboine River into Lake Manitoba, causing a surge in water levels that resulted in damage to the First Nations communities. The $90 million settlement was meant to be distributed among some 7,000 recipients.[362]

In another example of the justice system settling conflicts between First Nations and the federal government, in June of 2019, Southern Alberta's Blood Tribe First Nation, the country's largest reserve, won part of its forty-year land claim battle against the federal government. The presiding judge, Justice Russel Zinn, considered evidence that included century-old government documents and maps, handwritten letters, and oral history from Indigenous elders. The justice found that the band did not get all of the land promised by Canada, based on population under Treaty 7. The First Nation was entitled to 710 square miles of land as compared to the 547.5 square miles it had received.[363]

In another case involving the Blood Tribe, following a 2000 court challenge, the First Nation was awarded $150 million to settle its claim of the Crown's mismanagement of its cattle ranching assets from 1894 to 1923. The claim established that the government mismanaged the herd by failing to feed it adequately and by selling the cattle for less than half of their normal value. In a statement concerning the settlement, Crown-Indigenous Relations Minister Carolyn Bennett said: "We are sorry. Settling claims is the right thing to do."[364,365]

Recognition of wrongdoing and apologies by governments for their inappropriate actions have been made and continue to be made to affected communities. However, the fear remains. How can we prevent such actions from happening again? In the case of Canada's Indigenous Peoples, The Truth and Reconciliation Commission of Canada's report titled "A Knock on the Door" provides a way forward by enumerating a list of "Calls to Action." The National Inquiry into Missing and Murdered Indigenous Women and Girls has provided an opportunity for those families who have been affected to share their stories and for the general public to hear them. It has now become the practice to publicly acknowledge Canada's treaties with First Nations and also the role of Metis peoples in Canada's development.

Recent events may suggest some change in attitude toward voluntary, non-obligatory actions, although these announcements were made just a few months before a scheduled federal general election. In one such case, after many years of lobbying, a community group called the Regina Indian Industrial School Commemorative Association obtained title to a one-acre parcel of land six kilometres north of Regina, Saskatchewan. The site contains some thirty-five graves of Indigenous children who died while attending the Industrial school. The school operated from 1891 to 1910 and was attended by over 500 children. The children, buried in unmarked graves, were from First Nation and Metis communities in Alberta, Saskatchewan, and Manitoba. The land was transferred from the RCMP to the community group on June 25, 2019.[366]

In another case, on October 28, 2019, the Saskatchewan government declared the Battleford Industrial School Cemetery a provincial heritage site. The Battleford Industrial School was established in 1883 and was one of the first industrial schools established in Canada. It operated until 1914 and was superseded by a residential school established at Battleford. At least seventy-four people, most of them children who died while attending the school, are buried in the cemetery. The school was operated by the Anglican Church on behalf of the federal government. Gene Makowsky, Minister of Parks, Culture and Sport stated in a press release: "Commemorating those who lost their lives, language and culture through residential schools is an important step for our province on the path toward reconciliation."[367,368]

Agreements reached after decisions by the courts are also a step forward. On June 25, 2019, the federal government signed self-governing agreements with three provincial branches of the Metis Nations in Ontario, Alberta, and Saskatchewan. The self-governing agreements are the result of Supreme Court of Canada decisions that formally recognized Metis Aboriginal rights and the federal government's responsibility for issues affecting the Metis peoples. [369] The agreements do not include specific areas of jurisdiction such as child care, education, and administration of justice that affect the Metis, but they do provide a vehicle for negotiations. The agreements, to become law, were subject to approval by the House of Commons.

In another case, the federal government announced it is paying nine Saskatchewan First Nations $38.5M for $5 treaty payments that were withheld during the conflicts that occurred 1885 and 1888. The agreements were reached with the nine First Nations between May 2018 and January 2019 but not announced until July 2019.[370]

One positive sign that there may be a change in recognizing First Nation's concern respecting damage to Canada's natural resources occurred on December 20, 2019, when Nova Scotia Premier Stephen McNeil announced that his government would not allow Northern Pulp to continue to dump polluting waste into Boat Harbour near Pictou Landing First Nation. The government's decision could potentially affect some 3,000 jobs in the province's forest industry. Pictou Landing First Nation's Chief Andrea Paul stated: "Cleaning up Boat Harbour is all my people have wanted and Premier McNeil kept his promise and – on behalf of my community –we are thankful."[371]

Social Engineering and Internal Colonialism

To many Canadians, it may be a surprise to learn that the Canadian government and Canadian institutions have practised what can be described as social engineering and, moreover, that it still may be going on. As noted earlier, reports of sterilization of Indigenous women without their consent have surfaced over the last year.

The relocation of the Quebec Inuit to the High Arctic, the relocation of the Nunavut Ahiarmiut from the traditional lands, and the relocation of the Saysis Dene in Manitoba are examples of social engineering by the federal government. While the government gave different explanations for the relocations, the underlying reason was that the government thought it knew what was best for the people, whether they agreed with it or not. The results proved disastrous for the affected families and carried the trauma into future generations. The same type of trauma and family upheaval continues with respect to the implementation of the Indian Residential Schools, another case of social engineering where the government thought it knew best. In all three cases, the government was serving its interests and not those of the affected people.

Forcing unwed mothers to give up their babies for adoption, in this case with church support, is another example of social engineering by the government in Canada. Here again, those in authority decided what was best for the baby, traumatizing both the mothers and children as they grew into adulthood. The Sixties Scoop forced adoption of Indigenous children was motivated by the colonial attitude that governments and institutions know what is best for others.

The Internments and the War Measures Act

A far less subtle form of internal colonialism than social engineering were the internments of Canadian citizens. The two major internments occurred even though it had been determined, prior to full implementation, that they were unnecessary from a security point of view.

In the case of internments that took place during World War I, prejudice, economic factors, and political considerations played into the decisions to intern newly arrived immigrants who were mainly from central and eastern Europe. These immigrants arrived in Canada at the invitation of the Canadian government to develop and expand the Canadian economy, mostly in Western Canada. The recession, which started before the war, created unemployment and the need for the governments to provide welfare to the unemployed and largely unskilled workforce. This created resentment, which was stoked by newspaper editors, amongst the existing British-oriented population, many of whom carried the philosophy of keeping Canada "British." The result was that the Canadian government arrested and interned thousands of so-called "enemy aliens" in work camps across the country. The vehicle to do so was the War Measures Act, which allowed arrest and detention without due process and legal protection.

In the case of the internment of Japanese Canadians during World War II, prejudice was a major factor. According to Bill Waiser in his book *Park*

Prisoners, "The Japanese – all Asians, for that matter – had never been welcome in Canada's Pacific province, and through a series of restrictive policies and other discriminatory measures, had been relegated to the lower rungs of British Columbia's economy and society in the early twentieth century. They were segregated in urban and rural communities, largely confined to a few labour-intensive occupations, and generally prevented from integrating with the host society in any significant way. The dominant white population regarded the Japanese as a blot on the province's character and subjected them to pervasive racism that bordered on hatred. For most British Columbians, the Japanese were unassimilable, acquisitive, immoral and treacherous."[372]

The War Measures Act was adopted by Parliament in August 1914. It allowed the Federal Cabinet to arrest, jail, and intern people without recourse for the persons affected and without Parliamentary scrutiny. It was a perfect tool for a government to act with colonial authority and mindset. Following the passage of the Canadian Bill of Rights in 1960 and the October Crisis in 1970, when The War Measures Act was controversially used in Quebec to detain individuals without due process, it was repealed. It was replaced in 1998 with the Emergencies Act. In a positive development, the new Act limits the powers of the government in dealing with security emergencies with the result that the large-scale internments like those carried out during World Wars I and II will likely not occur again.

Racism, Prejudice, Discrimination, and Internal Colonialism

All of the examples of internal colonialism discussed in this book—the Indian Residential Schools, Sixties Scoop, removal of babies born to unwed mothers, internments, forced relocation of Inuit Peoples, and the treatment of First Nation Peoples—contain elements of racism, prejudice, and discrimination. Does this then mean that if internal colonialism is to be eliminated in Canada, that racism, prejudice, and discrimination will have to be eliminated as well? If the answer is yes, the way forward will be a daunting task.

Racism is embedded in our society. Black and Indigenous people are over-represented in our jails and are subject to greater suspicion by police than are white Canadians. Black and Indigenous Peoples do not generally attain the same education as does the white population, and many end up working in lower-paying jobs. Prejudice and discrimination against visible minority Canadians is ever-present—from rude treatment of a visible minority passenger on a transit bus in Montreal to the false accusation of an Indigenous man of shoplifting in a Regina store. The extent and level of racism and prejudice even reaches the highest level of government in Canada. In September 2019, three different photographs showed Prime Minister Justin Trudeau at three different events in blackface attire. In response to the photographs, Trudeau was quoted to say: "I take responsibility for my decision to do that. I shouldn't have done it. I should have known better. It was something I didn't think was racist at the time, but now I recognize it was something racist to do and I am deeply sorry." Trudeau was an adult in a position of some authority—twenty-nine years old and a high school teacher—when one of the photographs was taken. He blamed his "advantaged upbringing" for his actions.[373]

Any immediate decrease in racism in Canada is not evident. Results from Canada-wide surveys conducted in 2018 and 2019 show the country remained evenly divided when asked if racism was increasing or declining and if racism is a problem in Canada, suggesting there was no strong movement to combat racism in the country.[374,375] A report issued by the Ontario Human Rights Commission on August 10, 2020, found that Black people are more likely than others to be arrested, charged, or have force used against them during interactions with Toronto police. As an example, the study found that although Black people make up only 8.8 per cent of Toronto's population, they represent almost 32 per cent of people charged.[376] However, a possible first step in at least acknowledging racial discrimination against Black Canadians took place in Halifax on November 29, 2019, when the Halifax Police Chief publicly apologized to the city's Black community for the discriminatory street checks carried out by the police against them.[377] A second step in acknowledging the existence of racism in Canada was recorded in June 2020 in a poll conducted by Abacus Data. The Canada-wide survey was taken a number of months following the much-publicized killing of a Black man, George Floyd, by a police officer in Minneapolis. The poll showed that in Quebec and the Atlantic provinces, just over 50 percent think systemic racism exists in Canada. In Ontario and Alberta, the number was higher at 65 percent. In comparison to a similar poll conducted in 2016, the 2020 survey showed: "those thinking Black people were likely to experience 'a lot of' discrimination increased by nine percent, Indigenous people by seven percent, and people of Asian descent increased six percent." [378](2)

Where Does This Leave Us?

The many forms and instances of internal colonialism covered in this book span some 150 years of Canadian history. Some of these examples affected only dozens of people; in other instances, over 300,000 Canadians were affected. Some events lasted less than two years while other spanned over a hundred years. But, that was the past. Should we be concerned about the future?

Some progress has been made in eliminating internal colonialism in Canada. The repeal of the War Measures Act has reduced the possibility of jailing and interning Canadian citizens without due process. All Indian Residential Schools have been closed, and some affected students received compensation. There have been no recent known forced relocations of Indigenous People, although there have been discussions with respect to relocation of some northern First Nation communities. But some ideas associated with internal colonialism may remain. As recently as 1969, when Pierre Trudeau was prime minister and Jean Chrétien was Minister of Indigenous Affairs, the federal government produced the White Paper that recommended the suspension of all treaties signed with First Nations.[379]

There are two main areas in which internal colonialism is practised in Canada today. The first is largely centred within government institutions, such as the military, the RCMP, provincial and city police forces, health care organizations, and even within governments themselves. The second type of colonialism is centred on citizen groups such as Canada's Indigenous Peoples and people of colour where colonialism is manifested largely through racism, superiority, and discrimination.

In the case of internal colonialism practised within government institutions, it is ironic that citizens that have experienced colonialism in these organizations are forced to take to court the very institutions that were established to protect them. Governments and their institutions have shown strong reluctance to admit wrongdoing and seem to only do so when forced by the courts or as a reaction to lobbying by citizen groups.

Eliminating colonialism practised against citizen groups, in particular with Canada's Indigenous citizens and peoples of colour, will require changes in both attitudes and public policy. For example, the current approach by governments is largely to resolve issues through the courts. By doing so, the government is letting judges determine public policy rather than elected officials. Internal colonialism practised against Indigenous Peoples and people of colour is still widely manifest. And as noted earlier, racism is not declining in Canada. As a result of a series of events where the RCMP used questionable force against Indigenous men and only after considerable public pressure was applied, did the current RCMP Commissioner Brenda Lucki publicly acknowledge on June 12, 2020, that the RCMP did practice systemic racism against Canada's Indigenous Peoples and people of colour.[380]

Chapter 11
Afterword

THIS CHAPTER IDENTIFIES THREE EXAMPLES OF CRISES THAT COULD HAVE been avoided if governments had accepted their responsibility and were proactive rather than reactive in dealing with known issues. Loss of life, property damage, and continuing distrust could have been avoided.

Oka Crisis

The Oka Crisis was a seventy-eight-day standoff during the summer of 1990 between Mohawk First Nation protesters and the Quebec police and the Canadian Army near the city of Montreal. During the conflict period, one police officer was killed by a bullet and one fourteen-year-old First Nation girl was stabbed in the chest by a soldier's bayonet. Fear and mistrust between the First Nation communities and the police, military, and surrounding neighbourhoods continues to this day.

At the heart of the crisis was the proposed expansion of a golf course and development of condominiums on disputed land that included a Mohawk burial ground. The dispute over the land dates back to the 1700s, when the First Nation requested that the government give it ownership of the land, a request that was denied by succeeding governments. In 1961, a nine-hole golf course was built on land that, according to the Mohawk of the Kanesatake reserve, included a burial ground. In 1989, the mayor of Oka announced that the course would be expanded to eighteen holes and a sixty-unit condominium project would be built on the disputed land.

In order to stop the work from proceeding, a group of militants from the Kanesatake reserve, known as the Mohawk Warriors, constructed a barricade blocking access to the area. This group of protesters were later joined by Mohawks from two other reserves—Kahnawake and Akwesasne. The Quebec provincial police attacked the barricade using tear gas and concussion grenades. It was during this battle that Corporal Marcel Lemay of the Quebec provincial police was killed by an unidentified shooter.[381]

A month into the standoff, the Quebec premier brought in 800 members of the Canadian Armed Forces, and all of the barricades were dismantled. In the end, the golf course and condominium projects were cancelled, and the federal government bought all of the land in question. The government indicated that the land would be available for the Kanesatake Mohawks, but there was no formal transfer of the land.[382]

Ipperwash Crisis

In 1942, during the Second World War, the Canadian government planned to build an army training camp on the Stoney Point Reserve, located near Lake Huron, Ontario. When the federal government asked the Stoney Point First Nation to surrender their land for use as a training camp, they refused. The government, over the objections of the First Nation, then appropriated the land under the War Measures Act and relocated residents of the area to the nearby Kettle Point Reserve. While the government advised the First Nation that the use of their land, located near the Ipperwash Provincial Park, was only temporary, no action to return the land took place.

The Ipperwash Crisis took place in 1995. After repeated requests for their appropriated land to be returned, members of the Stoney Point First Nation occupied part of the army camp in 1993 and in 1995. On September 4, 1995, protesters also began occupation of the nearby Ipperwash Provincial Park in order to protect a burial ground they indicated was located there. With the occupation of the Park by the protesters, the provincial government ordered the Ontario Provincial Police to move in.

Tension in the area increased rapidly with the heavy police presence, which included the use of helicopters. Local media's unsubstantiated reports of gunfire further inflamed the situation. During the confusion,

Acting Sergeant Ken Deane shot Anthony O'Brian "Dudley" George, claiming that George had pointed a firearm at police officers. Deane was later convicted of criminal negligence causing death.[383]

The findings of an inquiry into the events at Ipperwash, conducted by Justice Sidney S. Linden, criticized the Ontario Provincial Police for failing to educate their officers regarding Indigenous rights and issues. The inquiry report also stated that the federal government had contributed to the tragic events by failing to return the land to the Stoney Point First Nation as was promised.[384] In April 2016, an agreement was signed that included the return of the land to the Kettle and Stoney Point First Nation, along with a $95 million compensation package.[385]

Wet'suwet'en Pipeline Conflict

In 2012, Coastal Gaslink began to plan the construction of a natural gas pipeline from Dawson Creek, BC, near the Alberta border, to Kitimat on the BC Pacific coast, where the gas would be liquefied and exported overseas by ship. Various applications to construct the pipeline to appropriate provincial authorities were made over the years; consultations were also held with First Nations. The pipeline route, some 670 kilometres long, passes through Wet'suwet'en territory that is occupied by a number of First Nations. These First Nations are governed by elected councils as well as by hereditary leaders.[386]

By 2019, Coastal Gaslink had received all necessary government approvals to proceed with construction and had agreement with five First Nations over whose land the pipeline passed. However, a number of hereditary chiefs objected to the pipeline route and set up roadblocks along the pipeline access road to block construction. The matter was deferred to the British Columbia Supreme Court, which issued an injunction prohibiting attempts to block construction.

The hereditary chiefs continued their objection to the pipeline location and gained national publicity and awareness of their position. The result was support by groups of First Nation members as well as others across the country that resulted in the blockage of railways, highways, and shipping facilities. The railway companies were the most affected and had to lay off substantial numbers of staff. After some three weeks of transportation disruption, there was concern about possible shortages of necessary goods and equipment.

Whether the hereditary chiefs are taking their position because of their genuine concern for the land or are taking their position for other reasons has yet to be determined. What is clear, however, is that First Nations across Canada hold a pent-up distrust of governments and resource developers.

These three examples of lost opportunities to avoid conflict by acting proactively instead of reacting to conflict situations illustrate the need for governments, government agencies, and others to abandon their colonial approach. The events described above were highly predictable. For example, in the case of the Wet'suwet'en pipeline, the conflict is very similar to the Tsilhqot'in conflict that occurred some 170 years previously in the same province of British Columbia. The main difference is that in the Tsilhqot'in case, the conflict was over a road crossing traditional First Nation territory. In the case of the Wet'suwet'en conflict, the dispute is over a pipeline crossing un-ceded First Nations territory.

Canadian Colonialism – An Ever-Present History

Colonialism, like racism, is deep-rooted. As one cannot fully understand the consequences of bullying, racism, discrimination, and prejudice until one has experienced them, the same can be said for colonialism. It is the hope that this book sheds light on the past, ongoing, and future consequences of internal colonialism in Canada for those who have and have not experienced it.

Acknowledgements

I WISH TO ACKNOWLEDGE AND THANK THE FOLLOWING FOR READING draft manuscripts, suggesting changes, and advising on sources of information and assistance.

Joe Dierker, Robert Doucette, Kathy Hardie, Dennis Johnson, Barbara Kishchuk, Dan Kishchuk, Marie Kishchuk, Paul Kishchuk, Tom Kishchuk, Nora Russel, Asit Sarkar, Lois Simmie, Frank Vella, Bill Waiser, and in particular, Natalie Kishchuk.

About the Author

BORIS KISHCHUK WAS BORN AND GREW UP IN SMALL-TOWN SASKATCHEWAN and attended the University of Saskatchewan in Saskatoon. His first three books – *Long-Term Care in Saskatchewan*, *Saskatchewan Crown Corporations*, and *Connecting with Ukraine* are centred on his home province. His fourth book, *Possessions*, is more reflective in nature, exploring why we do things that are destructive to ourselves and to others.

Canadian Colonialism, Past and Present identifies events in Canada's history that are not well-known, but they profoundly affected those Canadians who became involved.

Boris, with his wife Marie, lives in Saskatoon.

References

SECTION 1- Colonialism by Forced Uprooting and Displacement

Introduction: Canadian Colonialism

1 Stanford Encyclopedia of Philosophy, Colonialism, https://plato.stanford.edu/search/searcher.py?query=colonialism.

2 Jack Hicks. On the Application of Theories of 'Internal Colonialism' to Inuit Societies. Presentation for the Annual Conference of the Canadian Political Science Association Winnipeg, June 5, 2004; https://www.cpsa-acsp.ca/papers-2004/Hicks.pdf. Hicks notes two broad categories: 1. Internal colonialism as a domestic analogy to forms of economic and social domination in classical colonialism; and, 2. Internal colonialism as intra-national exploitation of distinct cultural groups (page 4). This definition is similar to what Nancy Shoemaker describes as "postcolonial colonialism": Nancy Shoemaker. A Typology of Colonialism. Perspectives on History, Oct 1, 2015; https://www.historians.org/publications-and-directories/perspectives-on-history/october-2015/a-typology-of-colonialism.

3 Oxford English Dictionary, Racism, https://www.oed.com/view/Entry/157097?redirectedFrom=racism#eid.

4 Bob Joseph. *21 Things You May Not Know About the Indian Act.* (Indigenous Relations Press, 2018), 107-114.

Chapter 1 – Indian Residential and Day Schools

5 M.R. Waters, S.L Forman, T.A Jennings. The Buttermilk Creek Complex and the Origins of Clovis at the Debra L. Friedkin Site, Texas. *Science.* 331. (24 March 2011): 1599–1603.

6 Alan D. McMillan. *Native Peoples and Cultures of Canada.* (Vancouver/Toronto: Douglas & McIntyre, 1988), 20.

7 Ibid, 3.

8 Stonechild, *The Knowledge Seekers,* 3-4.

9 Ibid, 63.

10 Blair Stonechild. The Knowledge Seekers. (Regina: University of Regina Press, 2016), 82.

[11] Historical Aboriginal Families. The Canadian Encyclopedia. Oct. 10, 2018.

[12] James Daschuk. *Clearing the Plains.* (Regina: University of Regina Press, 2013), 13.

[13] Ibid, 40.

[14] Ibid, 67.

[15] Ibid, 177.

[16] Cited in Ibid, 101.

[17] Cited in Ibid, 101.

[18] Government of Canada, Crown-Indigenous Relations and Northern Affairs Canada, Treaty texts, https://www.rcaanc-cirnac.gc.ca/eng/1370373165583/1581292088522. May 20, 2019.

[19] McMillan, 295.

[20] Government of Canada, Treaty texts, https://www.rcaanc-cirnac.gc.ca/eng/1370373165583/1581292088522, May 20, 2019.

[21] J.R. Miller. *Skyscrapers Hide the Heavens:* A History of Native-Newcomer Relations in Canada. (Toronto: University of Toronto Press, 2000, Third Edition), 218-219.

[22] McMillan, 296.

[23] Government of Canada, Ibid.

[24] Truth & Reconciliation Commission. A *Knock on the Door: The Essential History of Residential Schools from the Truth and Reconciliation Commission.* (Winnipeg: Truth & Reconciliation Commission and University of Manitoba Press, 2016), 19.

[25] Ibid, 19.

[26] Joseph, 116.

[27] Truth & Reconciliation Commission, 31.

[28] Ibid, 25.

[29] Joseph, 117.

[30] Truth & Reconciliation Commission, 25.

[31] Ibid, 29.

[32] Ibid, 30.

[33] Ibid, 32.

[34] Joseph. 1879, 169; 1880, 170; 1885, 171.

[35] Truth & Reconciliation Commission, 40.

[36] Ibid, 38.

[37] Ibid, 6.

[38] Ibid, 6.

[39] Joseph, 119.

[40] Ibid, 119.

[41] Ibid, 59.

[42] Ibid, 60.

[43] Ibid, 118.

[44] Truth & Reconciliation Commission, 7.

[45] Ibid, 38.

[46] Ibid,.35.

[47] Ibid, 9-16.

[48] Suzanne Fournier & Ernie Crey. *Stolen from Our Embrace.* (Vancouver/Toronto: Douglas & McIntyre, 1997), 47.

[49] Truth & Reconciliation Commission, 77.

[50] Ibid, 77.

[51] Ibid,.67.

[52] Theodore Fontaine. *Broken Circle:* The Dark Legacy of Indian Residential Schools: A Memoir. (Victoria: Heritage House Publishing, 2010), 125.

[53] Truth & Reconciliation Commission, 68.

[54] Ibid, 74.

[55] Ibid, 81.

[56] Ibid, 47.

[57] Ibid, 48-49.

[58] Ibid, 50.

[59] Ibid, 49.

[60] Raphael Victor Paul. *Beauval Indian Residential School 1944-1954: A Residential School Memoir.* (Saskatoon, Sk.: McNally Robinson Book Sellers. 2017), 72.

[61] Ibid, 71.

[62] Truth & Reconciliation Commission, 100.

[63] Ibid, 99.

[64] Ibid, 100.

[65] Ibid, 98-104.

[66] Ibid, 86-90.

[67] Ken S. Coates. *Best Left as Indians: Native-White Relations in the Yukon Territory, 1840-1973.* (Montreal: McGill-Queens University Press, 1991), 151.

[68] Paul, 51.

[69] Truth & Reconciliation Commission, 86-90.

[70] Ibid, 91.

[71] Fontaine, 13-14.

[72] Truth & Reconciliation Commission, 94.

[73] Ibid, 92.

[74] Ibid, 93.

[75] Ibid, 97.

[76] Ibid, 97.

[77] Miller, 130, 131, 133.

[78] Joseph, 90.

[79] Ibid, 124.

[80] Ibid, 85-86.

[81] Fontaine, 177-178, 188.

[82] Truth & Reconciliation Commission, 92-93.

[83] Amber Bernard, APTN News. Canada announces Indian Day Schools settlement, March 12 2019, https://aptnnews.ca/2019/03/12/canada-announces-indian-day-schools-settlement/.

[84] *Ottawa announces compensation of up to $200K for students of Indian Day Schools, $200M legacy fund.* CBC, March 12, 2019.

[85] *Federal Court approves Indian day school class-action settlement.* CBC. August 19, 2019.

Chapter 2 – Sixties Scoop – Forced Removal of Indigenous Children and Their Adoption

86 Telephone interview with Herman Rolfes, Minister of Health of Saskatchewan 1975-79. May 24 2019.

87 Marie Adams. *Our Son a Stranger: Adoption Breakdown and Its Effects on Parents.* (Montreal: McGill-Queens University Press, 2002).

88 James Sinclair and Sharon Dainard. *Sixties Scoop.* The Canadian Encyclopedia, Nov. 21, 2018, https://www.thecanadianencyclopedia.ca/en/article/sixties-scoop.

89 Suzanne Fournier & Ernie Crey. *Stolen from Our Embrace.* (Vancouver/Toronto: Douglas & McIntyre, 1997).

90 Aboriginal Justice Implementation Commission. *The Justice System and Aboriginal People: Report of the Aboriginal Justice Inquiry of Manitoba.* Chapter 14, Child welfare system, http://www.ajic.mb.ca/volumel/chapter14.html#6; citing Patrick Johnston, *Native Children and the Child Welfare System. Ottawa,* Ottawa, ON: Canadian Council on Social Development, 1983.

91 Edwin C. Kimelman et al., *No Quiet Place, Review Committee on Indian and Metis Adoptions and Placements* (Winnipeg: Manitoba Department of Community Services, 1985), 272–73.

92 Raven Sinclair, Raven. Identity Lost and Found: Lessons from The Sixties Scoop. *First Peoples Child and Family Review:* 3(1), 2007: 65-72, p. 66.

93 Fournier and Crey, 87.

94 Ibid, 90.

95 Ibid, 90.

96 Betty Ann Adams. *Scooped.* Reader's Digest. September, 2017: 93.

97 Colleen Cardinal. *Ohpikiihaakan-ohpihmeh (Raised somewhere else). A 60s Scoop Adoptee's Story of Coming Home.* (Halifax: Roseway Publishing, 2018).

98 Cardinal, 5.

99 Sinclair and Dainard, Ibid.

100 Ibid.

101 Megan McPhaden, CBC News. Sixties Scoop settlement the latest involving Canadian Indigenous people, October 7, 2017. https://www.cbc.ca/news/canada/government-canada-settlements-indigenous-1.4343541.

102 Government of Saskatchewan. *Sixties Scoop Apology,* January 7, 2019. https://www.saskatchewan.ca/government/news-and-media/2019/january/07/sixty-scoop-apology.

Chapter 3 – Unwed Mothers and Their Babies and Duplessis Orphans

103 National Post. *Forced Adoptions: curtain lifts on decades unwed mothers in Canada coerced into giving up children.* March 9, 2012. https://nationalpost.com/news/canada/curtain-lifts-on-decades-of-forced-adoptions-for-unwed-mothers-in-canada.

104 Standing Senate Committee on Social Affairs, Science and Technology, *The Shame is Ours; Forced Adoptions of the Babies of Unmarried Mothers in Post-war Canada.* July, 2018. https://sencanada.ca/en/info-page/parl-42-1/soci-adoption-mandate/.

[105] CBC Radio. *Women seek apology, inquiry, from government for forced adoption*. Dec. 2, 2018.

[106] Rahul Kalvapalle. 'The shame is ours': senate report chronicles forced adoptions in post-war Canada, Global News, https://global news.ca/news/4342569/forced-adoption-unmarried-women-canada-report/july 26, 2018. Dec. 2, 2018.

[107] Gloria Galloway, *Report calls on Ottawa to apologize to unwed mothers forced to give up babies after Second World War. Globe and Mail,* July 26, 2018. Dec. 2, 2018, https://www.theglobeandmail.com/politics/article-ottawa-urged-to-apologize-to-unwed-mothers-forced-to-give-up-babies/.

[108] National Post. *Forced Adoptions: curtain lifts on decades unwed mothers in Canada coerced into giving up children*. Nov. 27, 2018.

[109] Standing Senate Committee on Social Affairs, Science and Technology, Ibid.

[110] Canadian Encyclopedia of Human Rights. Duplessis Orphans, https://historyofrights.ca/encyclopaedia/main-events/duplessis-orphans/.

[111] As reported in Wikipedia, Duplessis orphans, October 30 2019, citing Moore, Lynne, Duplessis Orphans: Church, government cashed in, report says," *Montreal Gazette*, 27 April 1999, A5; "They deserve better" [editorial], *Montreal Gazette*, 28 April 1999, B2.

[112] P. Sigal, V. Perry, M., Rossignol, M-C. Ouimet. Unwanted Infants: Psychological and Physical Consequences of Inadequate Orphanage Care 50 Years Later. *American Journal of Orthopsychiatry,* 73(1) (2003): 3-12.

[113] The Canadian Encyclopedia. *Duplessis Orphans*. October 30, 2019.

Chapter 4 – World War I and World War II Internment

[114] Denis Smith, Richard Foot, Eli Yarhi, The Canadian Encyclopedia. *War Measures Act*. July 25 2018.

[115] Supreme Court (Canada), *Reference as to the Validity of the Regulations in Relation to Chemicals Enacted by Order in Council and of an Order of the Controller of Chemicals Made Pursuant Thereto (The "Chemicals Reference")* 1943 CanLII 1 at 17–18, [1943] SCR 1, January 1943 https://www.canlii.org/en/ca/scc/doc/1943/1943canlii1/1943canlii1.html.

[116] Lubomyr Luciuk, Kassandra Luciuk, The Canadian Encyclopedia. *Ukrainian Internment in Canada*. June 5, 2018

[117] Robert Craig Brown, Gord MacIntosh, The Canadian Encyclopedia. National Policy, March 4 2015, https://www.thecanadianencyclopedia.ca/en/article/national-policy.

[118] Luciuk and Luciuk, Ibid.

[119] Ibid.

[120] Wikipedia. *Battle of Cut Knife*. Feb. 4, 2019, citing among others, Charles Pelham Mulvaney, *The history of the North-West Rebellion of 1885 (Battle of Cut Knife Creek)*, (Toronto: A.H. Hovey & Co, 1985), 156, and noting sources are unreliable.

[121] Bohdan S. Kordan. *No Free Man: Canada, the Great War, and the Enemy Alien Experience*. (Montreal: McGill-Queen's University Press, 2016), 134.

[122] Sandra Semchuk. *The Stories Were Not Told: Canada's First World War Internment Camps*. (Edmonton: University of Alberta Press, 2019), 7.

[123] Luciuk and Luciuk, Ibid.

[124] Ibid.

[125] Kordan, 185.

[126] Internment Canada. Remembering Canada's First National Internment Operations. 1914 – 1920. G. *Willrich. Report to US Secretary of State. December 29, 1916.* https://www.internmentcanada.ca/PDF/CFWWIRF_Pamphlet_English.pdf.

[127] The Canadian Encyclopedia. Ukrainian Internment in Canada, Feb. 14, 2019.

[128] Ibid, Feb. 15, 2019.

[129] Semchuk, 95.

[130] Ibid, 96.

[131] Ibid, 101-102.

[132] Ibid, 104.

[133] Semchuk, 113.

[134] Ibid, 183.

[135] Ibid, 183.

[136] Internment Canada *The Redress Endowment*. The Ukrainian Weekly, 27 September 2009 https://www.internmentcanada.ca/PDF/articles/THE%20REDRESS%20ENDOWMENT.pdf.

[137] Luciuk and Luciuk, Ibid.

[138] Luciuk and Luciuk, Ibid.

[139] Lubomyr Luciuk, The Canadian Encyclopedia. Filip Konowal, VC. May 25, 2015, https://www.thecanadianencyclopedia.ca/en/article/filip-konowal.

[140] Canadian War Museum. *Enemy Aliens – The Internment of Canadian Ukrainians. Canada and the First World War*. Feb. 16, 2019, https://www.warmuseum.ca/firstworldwar/history/life-at-home-during-the-war/enemy-aliens/the-internment-of-ukrainian-canadians/.

[141] Marsh, James. The Canadian Encyclopedia. *Japanese Canadian Internment: Prisoners in their own Country*. Retrieved December 18 2018.

[142] Pamela Hickman & Masako Fukawa. *Righting Canada's Wrongs: Japanese Canadian Internment in the Second World War.* (Toronto: James Lorimer & Company, 2011), 14.

[143] Ibid, 17.

[144] Ibid, 18.

[145] Wikipedia. Japanese Canadian Internment. December 8, 2018, citing La Violette, Forrest E. *The Canadian Japanese and World War II: A Sociological and Psychological Account*. (Toronto: University of Toronto Press, 1948), 17.

[146] Ibid.

[147] Ibid.

[148] Hickman &Fukawa, 32. 2

[149] Wikipedia. Japanese Canadian Internment. December 8, 2018, citing La Violette, Forrest E. *The Canadian Japanese and World War II: A Sociological and Psychological Account*. (Toronto: University of Toronto Press, 1948), 24-25.

[150] Japanese Canadian Internment. Wikipedia. December 10, 2018, Citing Sunahara, Ann. The Politics of Racism: The Uprooting of Japanese Canadians During the Second World War. (Toronto: Lorimer, 1981).

[151] Ibid.

[152] Ibid.

[153] Ibid.

[154] Wikipedia. Japanese Canadian Internment. December 10, 2018, Citing Maryka Omatsu. *Bittersweet Passage: Redress and the Japanese Canadian Experience.* (Toronto: Between the Lines Press, 1992), 73.

[155] Ibid, December 10, 2018, Citing Sunhara, 47-48.

[156] Wikipedia. Japanese Canadian Internment. December 10, 2018, Citing Linda de Biase. Japanese Canadian Internment. Archived 2007-06-13, University of Washington Libraries, https://web.archive.org/web/20070613054742/http:/www.lib.washington.edu/subject/Canada/internment/intro.html.

[157] Hickman & Fukawa, 87.

[158] Ibid, 83.

[159] Ibid, 94.

[160] Ibid, 101.

[161] Ibid, 103.

[162] Hickman & Fukawa, 123.

[163] Takeo Nakano. *Within the barbed wire fence: A Japanese Man's Account of his Internment in Canada.* (Toronto: James Lorimer & Company Ltd., 2012).

[164] Ibid, 9.

[165] Hickman & Fukawa, 124.

[166] Ibid, 26.

[167] Ann Sunahara, 2012. As cited in Mona Oikawa, *Cartographies of Violence: : Japanese Canadian Women, Memory, and the Subjects of the Internment.* (Toronto: University of Toronto Press, 2012), 5.

[168] Ibid, 22.

[169] CBC Archives. *Canadian government apologises to Italian Canadians for wartime internment*, Sept. 22 1988, https://www.cbc.ca/archives/government-apologizes-to-japanese-canadians-in-1988-1.4680546.

[170] Hickman & Fukawa, 147.

[171] Daniela DiStefano. **T***racing the Forgotten History of Italian-Canadian Internment Camps,* https://www.panoramitalia.com/index.php/2012/08/13/tracing-the-forgotten-history-of-italian-canadian-internment-camps/, 2012.

[172] CBC Archives, *Apology to interned Italian Canadians questioned,* May 7, 2010. https://www.cbc.ca/news/canada/ottawa/apology-to-interned-italian-canadians-questioned-1.971511.

[173] Columbus Centre. *Italian Canadians as Enemy aliens: memories of WWII. Redress and apology,* http://www.italiancanadianww2.ca/theme/detail/redress_apology.Toronto.

[174] The Canadian Press. *Ottawa to issue apology to Italian Canadians mistreated during Second World War.* June 17, 2019, https://toronto.citynews.ca/2019/06/14/ottawa-to-issue-apology-to-italian-canadians-mistreated-during-second-world-war/.

[175] J. Nolan Reilly, The Canadian Encyclopedia. *The Winnipeg General Strike of 1919.* Feb. 26, 2019.

[176] William Repka and Kathleen Repka. Dangerous Patriots: Canada's Unknown Prisoners of War. (Vancouver: New Star Books, 1982).

[177] Theresa Miedema. University of Toronto Libraries Exhibit for 2016-2017 TRN 304Y "Law and Social Issues" class. *Canadian Wrongs: Jehovah's Witnesses Declared an "Illegal Operation,"* https://exhibits.library.utoronto.ca/exhibits/show/canadianlawandidentity/cdnwrongshome/cdnwrongswitnesses1. March 10 2020.

Chapter 5 - Forced Relocation – Quebec Inuit, the Nunavut Ahiarmiut and the Manitoba Sayisi Dene

[178] Nunavut Tunngavik Inc. *The High Arctic Relocations*, 2009. http://www.tunngavik.com/documents/publications/Naniiliqpita%20Fall%202009.pdf.

[179] Royal Commission on Aboriginal Peoples. *Report of the Royal Commission on Aboriginal Peoples.* The High Arctic Relocation. (Ottawa: Canada Communications Group, 1994), 10-11.

[180] Melanie McGrath. *The Long Exile: A Tale of Inuit Betrayal and Survival in the High Arctic.* (London: Fourth Estate, 2006), 48-49.

[181] Royal Commission on Aboriginal Peoples, 13.

[182] Ibid, 16.

[183] Ibid, 79.

[184] Ibid, 95.

[185] Ibid, 96.

[186] Ibid, 99.

[187] Royal Commission on Aboriginal Peoples, 17, 34, 35, 36.

[188] Ibid, 38-47.

[189] Ibid, 124.

[190] Ibid, 132-133.

[191] Ibid, 122-126

[192] Ibid, 132.

[193] Melanie McGrath, 287.

[194] Gerald I. Kenney. *Arctic Smoke and Mirrors.* (Prescott, Ontario: Voyageur Publishing, 1994), 9.

[195] Alan R. Marcus. Out in the Cold: The Legacy of Canada's Relocation Experiment in the High Arctic. (Copenhagen: International Working Group for Indigenous Affairs, 1992), 5.

[196] Ibid, 73.

[197] Ibid, 74.

[198] McGrath, 282-285.

[199] Royal Commission on Aboriginal Peoples.

[200] Wikipedia. *High Arctic Relocation.* Dec. 30, 2018, citing Matt James (2008*). "Wrestling with the Past: Apologies, Quasi-Apologies and Non-Apologies in Canada"*. In Mark Gibney, Rhoda E. Howard-Hassmann, Jean-Marc Coicaud and Niklaus Steiner (Eds.). *The Age of Apology*. (Philadelphia: University of Pennsylvania Press, 2008), 142–144.

[201] CBC News archive. Inuit get federal apology for forced relocation, Aug. 18 2010, https://www.cbc.ca/news/canada/north/inuit-get-federal-apology-for-forced-relocation-1.897468.

[202] Wikipedia. *Ihalmuit* Jan. 24, 2019, citing Farley Mowat, *No Man's River*. (Toronto: Key Porter Books, 2004).

[203] Ibid.

[204] Karine Duhamel and Warren Bernauer. *Ahiarmiut relocations and the search for justice.* Northern Public Affairs, 6(1), Jan. 25, 2019, https://www.northernpublicaffairs.ca/index/volume-6-issue-1/ahiarmiut-relocations-and-the-search-for-justice/.

[205] Frank James Tester and Peter Kulchyski. *Tammarniit (Mistakes):Inuit Relocation in the Eastern Arctic, 1939-63.* (Vancouver: UBC Press, 1994), 228.

[206] Ibid, 228.

[207] Government of Canada. *Statement of Apology for the Relocation of the Ahiarmiut,* Jan. 26, 2019, https://www.rcaanc-cirnac.gc.ca/eng/1548170252259/1548170273272.

[208] Ibid.

[209] Ibid.

[210] Alex Brockman, CBC News. Ottawa to apologize for forced relocation of Ahiarmiut in Nunavut Jan. 16, 2019, https://www.cbc.ca/news/canada/north/federal-government-apology-ahiarmiut-forced-relocation-1.4980762.

[211] Kelly Malone, CBC. *News Manitoba's Sayisi Dene: Forced relocation, racism, survival.*, August 16, 2016, https://www.cbc.ca/news/canada/manitoba/manitoba-sayisi-dene-relocation-1.3722564.

[212] Ibid.

[213] Virginia Phyllis Petch. *Relocation and loss of homeland, the story of the Sayisi Dene of Northern Manitoba.* Thesis presented to the University of Manitoba in partial fulfillment of the requirements of a Doctor of Philosophy in Anthropology. (Winnipeg: University of Manitoba, Winnipeg, 1998), http://www.collectionscanada.gc.ca/obj/s4/f2/dsk2/ftp02/NQ32015.pdf

SECTION 2: Colonialism by Direct Attack and Subjugation

Chapter 6 – Colonialism and its Deadly Consequences – the Tsilhqot'in War and the North-West Rebellion

[214] Mel Rothenburger. *The Chilcotin War: True Story of a Defiant Chief's Fight to Save his Land from White Civilization.* (Langley, B.C.: Mr. Paperback, 1978), 78.

[215] Ibid, 33.

[216] Ibid, 35.

[217] Mole, Rich. *The Chilcotin War: A Tale of Death and Reprisal.* (Surrey, BC: Heritage House, 2011), 70–128.

[218] Ibid.

[219] Ibid.

220 Tristin Hopper, National Post. *What really happened in the Chilcotin War, the 1864 conflict that just prompted an exoneration from Trudeau?* March 27, 2018, https://nationalpost.com/news/canada/what-really-happened-in-the-chilcotin-war-the-1864-conflict-that-just-prompted-an-exoneration-from-trudeau.

221 Ibid.

222 Ibid.

223 Rothenburger, 189.

224 Hopper, Ibid.

225 Ibid.

226 Ibid.

227 W. Stewart Wallace, Claude Bélanger. *North-West Rebellion.* Montreal, Québec History Encyclopedia, Marianopolis College, 1948). http://faculty.marianopolis.edu/c.belanger/quebechistory/encyclopedia/North-WestRebellion-CanadianHistory.htm.

228 Bob Beal, Rod Macleod, Richard Foot and Eli Yarhi, The Canadian Encyclopedia. *North-West Rebellion*. July 30, 2019, https://www.thecanadianencyclopedia.ca/en/article/north-west-rebellion.

229 Ibid.

230 Ibid.

231 Don McLean. *1885: Metis Rebellion or Government Conspiracy?* (Winnipeg: Pemmican Publications, 1985).

232 Charles Pelham Mulvaney, *The history of the North-West Rebellion of 1885 (The War Cloud Bursts on Battleford)* (Toronto: A.H. Hovey & Co, 1985), 76, http://peel.library.ualberta.ca/bibliography/1508/76.html.

233 Encyclopedia of Saskatchewan, Frog Lake Massacre. http://esask.uregina.ca/entry/frog_lake_massacre.html.

234 William Bleasdell Cameron. The war trail of Big Bear (The Fall of Fort Pitt). (Toronto: Ryerson Press, 1888). http://peel.library.ualberta.ca/bibliography/1360/129.html.

235 Wikipedia. *Battle of Cut Knife*. Feb. 4, 2019, citing among others, Charles Pelham Mulvaney, *The history of the North-West Rebellion of 1885 (Battle of Cut Knife Creek)*, (Toronto: A.H. Hovey & Co, 1985), 156, and noting sources are unreliable.

236 Parks Canada. *Canada's Historic Places: Frenchman Butte National Historic Site.* https://www.historicplaces.ca/en/rep-reg/place-lieu.aspx?id=14509&pid=0 https://www.pc.gc.ca/en/lhn-nhs/sk/frenchman https://www.pc.gc.ca/en/lhn-nhs/sk/frenchman/culture.

237 Bob Beal, Canadian Encyclopedia Steele Narrows Battle (Battle of Loon Lake), Feb. 5, 2019, https://archive.is/20131118094101/http://www.thecanadianencyclopedia.com/articles/steele-narrows-battle.

238 Ted McCoy. *Legal Ideology in the Aftermath of Rebellion: The Convicted First Nations Participants, 1885.* (Peterborough: Trent University, 2009), 184.

239 Ibid.

240 Blair Stonechild and Bill Waiser. *Loyal till Death: Indians and the North-West Rebellion.* (Markham, Ontario: Fifth House Books, 2010), 261-263.

241 McCoy, 186.

242 Ibid, 201.

243 Frank Anderson. *The Riel Rebellion 1885.* (Calgary: Frontier Publishing, 1968), 69.

[244] Ibid, 68.

[245] Wallace and Belanger, Ibid

[246] Anderson, 68.

[247] Manitoba Historical Society, *Memorable Manitobans, Louis "David" Riel* http://www.mhs.mb.ca/docs/people/riel_l.shtml. March 6, 2019.

SECTION 3: Colonialism by Disdain, Disrespect and Denial of Rights

Chapter 7 - Colonialism by Neglect – Famine, Disease, Water Quality, Child Care and Social Services

[248] Wes Olson, The Canadian Encyclopedia. *Bison*. October 8, 2019, https://www.thecanadianencyclopedia.ca/en/article/bison.

[249] Ibid.

[250] James Daschuk. *Clearing the Plains*. (Regina: University of Regina Press, 2013), 74.

[251] Ibid, 101.

[252] Government of Canada, Crown-Indigenous Relations and Northern Affairs Canada, Treaty texts, Treaty No. 6, https://www.rcaanc-cirnac.gc.ca/eng/1100100028710/1581292569426.

[253] Indigenous Corporate Training Inc. *The Impact of Smallpox on First Nations on the West Coast.* October 7, 2019, https://www.ictinc.ca/blog/the-impact-of-smallpox-on-first-nations-on-the-west-coast.

[254] Ibid.

[255] Ibid.

[256] C. Stuart Houton and Stan Houston. The first smallpox epidemic on the Canadian Plains: In the fur-trader's words. The Canadian Journal of Infectious Diseases, 11(2), 2000: 112-5.

[257] Daschuk, 68.

[258] Daschuk, 60, 67, 68.

[259] Louis Bergeron, Stanford News Services. *Tuberculosis strain spreads by the fur trade reveals stealthy approach of epidemics, say Stanford researchers.* October 7, 2019, https://news.stanford.edu/news/2011/april/tuberculous-genetic-analysis-040711.html.

[260] Daschuk, 100.

[261] Ibid, 162.

[262] Ibid, 176.

[263] Canadian Public Health Association. *TB and Aboriginal people.* March 9, 2019, https://www.cpha.ca/tb-and-aboriginal-people.

[264] Ibid.

[265] CBC News. *Trudeau apologizes for "colonial, purposeful" mistreatment of Inuit with tuberculosis.* March 9, 2019, https://www.cbc.ca/news/canada/north/trudeau-apology-tuberculosis-iqaluit-1.5047805.

[266] Council of Canadians. *Federal party leaders urged to end drinking water crisis in First Nation communities once and for all.* Media Release. October 13, 2015, https://canadians.org/update/federal-party-leaders-urged-end-drinking-water-crisis-first-nation-communities-once-and-all.

[267] Government of Canada. Water on Reserves www.Canada.ca/water-on-reserves. Consulted June 19, 2019; link no longer functional; replaced by Water in First Nations communities, https://www.sac-isc.gc.ca/eng/1100100034879/1521124927588.

[268] Alastair Sharp, National Observer. *Decades after 1976 flood, Kashechewan First Nation still hopes to relocate.* June 19, 2019, https://www.nationalobserver.com/2019/05/01/news/decades-after-1976-flood-kashechewan-first-nation-still-hopes-relocate.

[269] Ben Spurr, The Star. How the Attawapiskat suicide crisis unfolded. July 27, 2019, https://www.thestar.com/news/canada/2016/04/18/how-the-attawapiskat-suicide-crisis-unfolded.html.

[270] CBC News. *Medical teams, new water systems part of federal commitment to Attawapiskat, chief says,* July 27, 2019, https://www.cbc.ca/news/canada/sudbury/feds-commit-attawapiskat-water-1.5218605

[271] Charnel Anderson, Canadian Encyclopedia. *Grassy Narrows.* https://www.thecanadianencyclopedia.ca/en/article/grassy-narrows; Wikipedia: *Asubpeeschoseewagong First Nation*. August 3, 2019.

[272] Olivia Stefanovich, CBC News. *Grassy Narrows chief to run for NDP in federal election.* August 3, 2019, https://www.cbc.ca/news/politics/grassy-narrows-chief-rudy-turtle-ndp-1.5228589.

[273] Natasha Beedie, David Macdonald, Daniel Wilson. *Towards Justice: Tackling Indigenous Child Poverty in Canada* (Ottawa: Assembly of First Nations, Upstream, and Canadian Centre for Policy Alternatives, 2019).

[274] Nicholas Keung, The Star.com. *Almost half of Status First Nations children live in poverty, study finds.* July 20, 2019, https://www.thestar.com/news/gta/2019/07/09/almost-half-of-status-first-nations-children-live-in-poverty-study-finds.html.

[275] APTN News. *Federal government challenging tribunal order to compensate First Nation children in care.* October 28, 2019, https://aptnnews.ca/2019/10/04/federal-government-challenging-tribunal-order-to-compensate-first-nations-children-in-care/.

[276] Ibid.

[277] Ibid.

[278] Public Inquiry Commission on relations between Indigenous Peoples and certain public services in Québec: listening, reconciliation and progress Final report, https://www.cerp.gouv.qc.ca/fileadmin/Fichiers_clients/Rapport/Final_report.pdf; CBC News, Sept. 30 2019, https://www.cbc.ca/news/canada/montreal/quebec-treatment-indigenous-viens-commission-report-1.5297888.

[279] Canadian Press, Oct. 2 2019. Quebec inquiry that examined treatment of Indigenous people calls for apology, https://cfjctoday.com/2019/10/02/quebec-inquiry-that-examined-treatment-of-indigenous-people-calls-for-apology/.

[280] Philip Authier, Montreal Gazette. *Premier formally apologizes to Indigenous Peoples in Quebec*, Oct. 2 2019, https://montrealgazette.com/news/quebec/premier-francois-legault-formally-apologizes-for-treatment-of-indigenous-peoples-in-quebec.

Chapter 8 – Colonialism by Embedded Racism

[281] Robyn Maynard. *Policing Black Lives: State Violence in Canada from Slavery to the Present*. (Halifax: Fernwood Publishing, 2017), 5.

[282] Ibid, 17.

[283] Joseph Mensah. *Black Canadians History, Experience, Social Conditions*. (Halifax: Fernwood Publishing, 2017), 46.

[284] Maynard, 20.

[285] Ibid, 20.

[286] Ibid, 21.

[287] Vic Satzewich. *Racism in Canada*. (Toronto: Oxford University Press, 2011), 35.

[288] Ibid, 35.

[289] Ibid, 39.

[290] Ibid, 39.

[291] Ibid, 45.

[292] James W. St.G. Walker, The Canadian Encyclopedia. *Black Canadians*. Jan. 10, 2019, https://www.thecanadianencyclopedia.ca/en/article/black-canadians.

[293] Maynard, 213.

[294] Ibid, 213.

[295] Ibid, 216.

[296] Ibid, 217.

[297] Mensah, 158.

[298] Maynard, 222.

[299] Mensah, 154-156.

[300] Ibid, 158-173.

[301] Carol Taylor and Frances Henry. *Racial Profiling in Canada*. (Toronto: University of Toronto Press. 2006), 88.

[302] Ibid, 88-89.

[303] Ibid, 88.

[304] Satzewich, 76.

[305] Ibid, 76.

[306] Maynard, 89.

[307] Phlis McGregor and Angela MacIvor, CBC News. *Black people 3 times more likely to be street checked in Halifax, police say*. January 15, 2019, https://www.cbc.ca/news/canada/nova-scotia/halifax-black-street-checks-police-race-profiling-1.3925251.

[308] Ontario Human Rights Commission. *A Collective Impact: Interim report on the inquiry into racial profiling and racial discrimination of Black persons by the Toronto Police Service*. 2018, http://ohrc.on.ca/sites/default/files/TPS%20Inquiry_Interim%20Report%20EN%20FINAL%20DESIGNED%20for%20remed_3_0.pdf#overlay-context=en/news_centre/

ohrc-interim-report-toronto-police-service-inquiry-shows-disturbing-results; The Globe and Mail. Black people more likely to be injured or killed by Toronto police officers, report finds. January 15, 2019.

309 Molly Hayes, The Globe and Mail. *Black people more likely to be injured or killed by Toronto police officers, report finds.* January 15, 2019, https://www.theglobeandmail.com/canada/toronto/article-report-reveals-racial-disparities-in-toronto-polices-use-of-force/.

310 CBC News. Black people in Halifax 6 times more likely to be street checked than whites. March 28, 2019, https://www.cbc.ca/news/canada/nova-scotia/street-checks-halifax-police-scot-wortley-racial-profiling-1.5073300.

311 Ontario Human Rights Commission. *Paying the Price: The Human Cost of Racial Profiling. Inquiry Report, 2003.* http://www.ohrc.on.ca/sites/default/files/attachments/Paying_the_price%3A_The_human_cost_of_racial_profiling.pdf.

312 Ontario Human Rights Commission. *Paying the Price: The Human Cost of Racial Profiling. Inquiry Report, 2003,* http://www.ohrc.on.ca/sites/default/files/attachments/Paying_the_price%3A_The_human_cost_of_racial_profiling.pdf.

313 Maynard, 91.

314 Satzewich, 70.

315 Ibid, 71.

316 Royal Canadian Mounted Police. *Working Together to End Violence Against Indigenous Women and Girls. National Scan of RCMP Initiatives.* May 17, 2017. Jan. 9, 2019, http://www.rcmp-grc.gc.ca/en/working-together-end-violence-indigenous-women-and-girls-national-scan-rcmp-initiatives-may-2017.

317 John Paul Tasker, CBC News. *Inquiry into missing and murdered Indigenous women issues final report with sweeping calls for change.* June 14, 2019, https://www.cbc.ca/news/politics/mmiwg-inquiry-deliver-final-report-justice-reforms-1.5158223.

318 National Inquiry into Missing and Murdered Indigenous Women and Girls. *Reclaiming Power and Place: Final Report, 2019* Vol. 1a, p. 50, https://www.mmiwg-ffada.ca/wp-content/uploads/2019/06/Final_Report_Vol_1a-1.pdf.

319 Adrian Humphreys, National Post. *Report on missing murdered Indigenous women call for significant changes to police services across Canada.* June 14, 2019, https://nationalpost.com/news/canada/report-on-missing-and-murdered-indigenous-women-and-girls-calls-for-significant-change-to-police-services-across-canada.

320 Ibid; see also National Inquiry into Missing and Murdered Indigenous Women and Girls. *Reclaiming Power and Place: Final Report,* 2019. Vol. 1a, p. 20, https://www.mmiwg-ffada.ca/wp-content/uploads/2019/06/Final_Report_Vol_1a-1.pdf.

321 Avery Zingel, CBC News. *Indigenous women come forward with accounts of forced sterilization, says lawyer.* June 16, 2019, https://www.cbc.ca/news/canada/north/forced-sterilization-lawsuit-could-expand-1.5102981.

322 Courtney Parker. *An Act of Genocide: Canada's Coerced Sterilization of First Nations Women.* Intercontinental Cry, November 2018, https://intercontinentalcry.org/canadas-coerced-sterilization-of-first-nations-women/.

323 Zingel, Ibid.

[324] Kristy Kirkup, Canadian Press. *RCMP seeking names of potential victims of coerced sterilization, commissioner says,* https://globalnews.ca/news/5406369/rcmp-coerced-sterlization/.

[325] Kristy Kirkup, Canadian Press. *Committee "deeply disturbed" by reports of coerced, forced sterilization.* August 7, 2019, https://www.cbc.ca/news/canada/edmonton/house-of-commons-committee-coerced-sterilization-1.5238521.

[326] Adam Gaudry, *Metis.* Sept.11, 2019. – The Canadian Encyclopedia, https://www.thecanadianencyclopedia.ca/en/article/metis.

[327] Jean Teillet, The North-West is Our Mother. (New York: Harper Collins Publisher Ltd. 2019), 473-484.

[328] Statistics Canada. First Nations People, Metis and Inuit in Canada: Diverse and Growing Populations. March 28, 2018.

[329] Jean Teillet. 183

[330] Adam Gaudry, *Metis.* The Canadian Encyclopedia.

[331] Jean Teillet. 277.

[332] J.E. Rea & Jeff Scott, *Manitoba Act.* The Canadian Encyclopedia. April 6 2016, https://www.thecanadianencyclopedia.ca/en/article/manitoba-act.

[333] Amanda Robinson, *Metis Scrip in Canada,* November 6 2018, https://www.thecanadianencyclopedia.ca/en/article/metis-scrip-in-canada.

[334] E. Rea & Jeff Scott, *Manitoba Act.* The Canadian Encyclopedia.

[335] Ossie Michelin. *Canadian Inuit Dog.* The Canadian Encyclopedia. Nov. 28, 2019, https://www.thecanadianencyclopedia.ca/en/article/canadian-inuit-dog.

[336] Ibid.

[337] Sara Minogue. Investigation into sled dog slaughter also an amazing historical record. CBC News. May 5, 2019, https://www.cbc.ca/news/canada/north/sara-minogue-inuit-dog-slaughter-1.5116972.

[338] The Canadian Press. Federal government apologizes to Inuit for historic sled dogs killing in the North. The Globe and Mail. August 14, 2019, https://www.theglobeandmail.com/canada/article-federal-government-apologizes-for-historic-sled-dog-killings-in-the-2/.

[339] Richard J. Brennan. Inuit communities finally get compensation for dog slaughter. The Star. June 27, 2013,. https://www.thestar.com/news/canada/2012/06/29/inuit_communities_finally_get_compensation_for_dog_slaughter.html#:~:text=Residents%20of%20Nunavik%20in%20northern,that%20left%20Inuit%20communities%20devastated.

[340] Kirk Macken. What really happened to the Inuit sled dogs? The Globe and Mail. July 5, 2005, https://www.theglobeandmail.com/news/national/what-really-happened-to-the-inuit-sled-dogs/article983351/.

[341] Arlene Chan, The Canadian Encyclopedia. *The Chinese Head Tax in Canada.* Jan. 20, 2019, https://www.thecanadianencyclopedia.ca/en/article/chinese-head-tax-in-canada.

[342] Charmaine Noronha, Huffington Post. *This Chinese Canadian Vet Fought in WWII and Battled Racism on Home Soil.* May 29, 2019, https://www.huffingtonpost.ca/entry/chinese-canadian-veterans-wwii_ca_5cdf0d10e4b09e057803c38a?guccounter=1&guce_referrer=aHR0cHM6Ly93d3cuZ29vZ2xlLmNvbS8&guce_referrer_sig=AQAAAKUU_hOMe16RuO74fO4UTuuQaTg0Y4XMEOLQi39-4XFuweC-

MonpSiqv1okpLG0RCAU-aIa5RjokV1CyF0_Ij8g8ucUm6cbA_hbqRuP2KIBXD4kh6_ipgYmx79KEugVFcl8ceHi2oxQygOXweu-u9Fm83m6a2UZscy-qPnsdrWQZX.

343 Chan, Ibid.

Chapter 9 – Hidden Internal Colonialism Within the Military, Police Forces and Public Services

344 Richard Burnett. *Looking back at Quebec queer life since the 17th century,* Xtra, https://www.dailyxtra.com/looking-back-at-quebec-queer-life-since-the-17th-century-30878.

345 Hamish. *"Sodomites" in Canada before 1841.* The Drummer's Revenge, August 19 2007, https://thedrummersrevenge.wordpress.com/2007/08/19/sodomites-in-canada-before-1841/.

346 Dan Levin, New York Times. *Canada Offers $85 Million to Victims of Its 'Gay Purge,' as Trudeau Apologizes.* November 28 2017, https://www.nytimes.com/2017/11/28/world/canada/canada-apology-gay-purge-compensation.html.

347 Jim Bronskill, Canadian Press. *Canada to compensate 718 gay-purge victims in class-action settlement.* July 13, 2019, https://nationalpost.com/news/canada/canada-to-compensate-718-gay-purge-victims-in-class-action-settlement.

348 Levin, Ibid.

349 Andrea Woo, The Globe and Mail. Six RCMP officers who spoke about sexual harassment. July 16, 2019, https://www.theglobeandmail.com/news/national/six-rcmp-officers-who-spoke-out-about-sexual-harassment/article32287259/.

350 Ashifa Kassam, The Guardian. Royal Canadian Mounted Police apologizes for sexual harassment. October 26, 2016, https://www.theguardian.com/world/2016/oct/06/royal-canadian-mounted-police-sexual-harassment-apologises.

351 Rhianna Schmunk, CBC News. *New $100M settlement reached in RCMP sexual harassment case.* July 8, 2019, https://www.cbc.ca/news/canada/british-columbia/rcmp-sexual-harassment-lawsuit-100-million-settlement-1.5203683.

352 Brian Hill, Global News. *Number of RCMP sexual harassment, discrimination claims rises to 2,400 women.* January 26, 2018.

353 Catharine Tunney, CBC News. *Ottawa sets aside $900M to settle sexual misconduct lawsuits against Canadian Armed Forces.* July 18, 2019, https://www.cbc.ca/news/politics/military-sexual-misconduct-settlement-1.5216307.

354 CTV News. *Veterans to sue gov't over military-issued-drug.* December 18, 2018, https://www.ctvnews.ca/health/it-stole-my-life-veterans-to-sue-gov-t-over-military-issued-drug-1.4223724.

355 Avery Haines, CTV-W5. *Canadian veterans suing government over anti-malaria drug's adverse effects.* October 20, 2019, https://www.ctvnews.ca/w5/canadian-veterans-suing-government-over-anti-malarial-drug-s-adverse-effects-1.4402691.

SECTION 4: Conclusion

Chapter 10 – Canadian Colonialism – Past and Present

[356] J. R. Miller. *Residential Schools and Reconciliation: Canada Confronts its History.* (Toronto: University of Toronto Press, 2017), 265.

[357] Ibid, 265-266.

[358] Interview with Sid Fiddler. Saskatoon, SK. July 23, 2018.

[359] Alanna Rizza, Canadian Press. *First Nations win case over $4 benefit from Queen's Park,* Ottawa. December 27, 2018.

[360] Sean Fine, Globe and Mail. *Court ruling to grant First Nations a much bigger cut of resources royalties in Ontario, January 4,* 2019, https://www.theglobeandmail.com/canada/article-court-ruling-to-grant-first-nations-a-much-bigger-cut-of-resources/.

[361] Rizza, Ibid.

[362] Steve Lambert. The Canadian Press. *Judge approves $9M settlement for flooded Manitoba First Nations.* January 12, 2018, https://www.theglobeandmail.com/news/national/judge-approves-90-million-settlement-for-flooded-manitoba-first-nations/article37596124/.

[363] Meghan Grant, CBC News. *Blood Tribe wins massive land claim battle in Federal Court.* June 12, 2019, https://www.cbc.ca/news/canada/calgary/blood-tribe-big-land-claim-federal-court-decision-1.5172198.

[364] Sarah Rieger, CBC News. *Blood Tribe members to vote on historic $150M cattle mismanagement settlement from Ottawa.* March 11, 2019, https://www.cbc.ca/news/canada/calgary/blood-tribe-cattle-settlement-vote-1.5050861.

[365] CBC News. "*'This was one of many wrongs that were done': Blood Tribe settles $150 million historic cattle claim,*" https://www.cbc.ca/news/canada/calgary/blood-tribe-announcement-1.5200946. July 18, 2019.

[366] CBC News. *First step in reconciliation as government hands over residential school cemetery. Saskatchewan.* June 25, 2019, https://www.cbc.ca/news/canada/saskatchewan/riis-residential-school-cemetery-land-transfer-1.5188585.

[367] BattlefordsNOW Staff. *Battleford Industrial School Cemetery receives provincial heritage property designation.* October 28, 2010, https://battlefordsnow.com/2019/10/28/battleford-industrial-school-cemetery-receives-provincial-heritage-property-designation/.

[368] CBC News. *Battleford Industrial School Cemetery now a provincial heritage site.* October 28, 2019, https://www.cbc.ca/news/canada/saskatchewan/battleford-industrial-school-cemetery-heritage-property-1.5338494.

[369] Government of Canada, News Release. *Historic self-government agreements signed with the Métis Nation of Alberta, the Métis Nation of Ontario and the Métis Nation-Saskatchewan,* June 26, 2019, https://www.canada.ca/en/crown-indigenous-relations-northern-affairs/news/2019/06/historic-self-government-agreements-signed-with-the-metis-nation-of-alberta-the-metis-nation-of-ontario-and-the-metis-nation-saskatchewan.html.

[370] CBC News. *Settlements between Ottawa and 9 Sask. First Nations for missed 1880s treaty payments, total $38.5M.* July 21, 2019, https://www.cbc.ca/news/canada/saskatchewan/ottawa-settlement-with-saskatchewan-first-nations-1.5218716.

[371] CTV News Atlantic. N.S. *premier rejects mill's plea for time. 'There will be no extension'* December 20, 2019, https://atlantic.ctvnews.ca/n-s-premier-rejects-mill-s-plea-for-time-there-will-be-no-extension-1.4738291.

[372] Bill Waiser. *Park Prisoners: The Untold Story of Western Canada's National Parks, 1915-1946.* (Saskatoon: Fifth House Publishers, 1999), 176-178.

[373] CBC News. *What we know about Justin Trudeau's blackface photos – and what happens next.* September 20, 2019, https://www.cbc.ca/news/politics/canada-votes-2019-trudeau-blackface-brownface-cbc-explains-1.5290664.

[374] Roberta Rocha, CBC News. *Quebeckers among Canadians most likely to believe racism is decreasing.* November 23, 2018, https://www.cbc.ca/news/canada/montreal/quebecers-among-canadians-most-likely-to-believe-racism-is-decreasing-1.4887461.

[375] Maham Abedi, Global News. *Canadian's view on racism unchanged, despite difficult conversations in 2019: poll.* January 10, 2020, https://globalnews.ca/news/6321879/canada-racism-blackface-don-cherry/.

[376] Adam Carter. CBC News. *Black people face "disproportionately" high charge, arrest rates from Toronto police: report.* August 10, 2020, https://www.cbc.ca/news/canada/toronto/black-people-human-right-commission-police-1.5680460.

[377] Michael Tutton, Global News. *Halifax police apologizes to black community for street checks.* Nov. 29, 2019, https://globalnews.ca/news/6232971/halifax-police-chief-apology-street-checks-2/[377] Roberta Rocha, CBC News. *Quebeckers among Canadians most likely to believe racism is decreasing.* November 23, 2018, https://www.cbc.ca/news/canada/montreal/quebecers-among-canadians-most-likely-to-believe-racism-is-decreasing-1.4887461.

[377] Maham Abedi, Global News. *Canadian's view on racism unchanged, despite difficult conversations in 2019: poll.* January 10, 2020, https://globalnews.ca/news/6321879/canada-racism-blackface-don-cherry/.

[377] Michael Tutton, Global News. *Halifax police apologizes to black community for street checks.* Nov. 29, 2019, https://globalnews.ca/news/6232971/halifax-police-chief-apology-street-checks-2/.

[378] *Almost two-thirds of Canadians believe systemic racism exists in the country: poll.* July 21, 2020. City News Toronto, https://toronto.citynews.ca/2020/06/11/racism-discrimination-canada-poll/.

[379] Bob Joseph. *21 Things You May Not Know About the Indian Act.* (Neyaashiinigmiing:Indigenous Relations Press, 2018), 89-91.

[380] RCMP Commissioner Brenda Lucki acknowledges systematic racism in the police force. CTV News/ June 16, 2020, https://www.ctvnews.ca/canada/lucki-acknowledges-systemic-racism-in-rcmp-1.4982165.

[381] Tabitha Marshall, The Canadian Encyclopedia, Oka Crisis, January 28, 2019, https://www.thecanadianencyclopedia.ca/en/article/oka-crisis.

[382] Ibid.

383 Tabitha Marshall, The Canadian Encyclopedia. *Ipperwash Crisis*. Feb. 6, 2019, https://www.thecanadianencyclopedia.ca/en/article/ipperwash-crisis.

384 Ibid.

385 Ibid.

386 Rafferty Baker, CBC News. A who's who of the Wet'suwet'en pipeline conflict, February 26, 2020, https://www.cbc.ca/news/canada/british-columbia/wetsuweten-whos-who-guide-1.5471898.

INDEX

Note the italicized "*n*" after certain page numbers relates to the endnote number.

A

B

C

E

F

G

H

M

O

P

Q

S

T

Printed in Canada